The Ever-Widening Circles

Marg Schrader

Philip
Garside
Publishing Ltd.

Email Marg at: margschrader.nz@gmail.com
Edited by Angela Robertson

Paperback International: ISBN 9781991027467

Also available
New Zealand paperback: ISBN 9781991027450
Paperback print-on-demand USA: ISBN 9798394975950
PDF: ISBN 9781991027474
ePub/Kindle/Mobi: ISBN 9781991027481

Philip Garside Publishing Ltd
PO Box 17160
Wellington 6147
New Zealand

books@pgpl.co.nz – www.philipgarsidebooks.com

Cover photograph:
Marg Schrader taken in 1995 when she was Moderator of the Presbyterian Church of Aotearoa New Zealand

Unless otherwise noted, all photographs and images in this book are from the author's collection

Contents

Foreword

Creation speaks to me.

Walking the beach – pondering my life with its ever-widening circles I came across a piece of wood. (See photo section) Richard Rohr, my favourite author, uses this image of the ever-widening circles to describe his life.

I recently went to an Association of Spiritual Directors (ACSD) weekend, during which I was asked to choose an acorn from a large group of them. Of course, I chose the one with a crack and no 'hat' on it. Aware of my age, 83, and so much older than the others at the conference, and a lack of a hat, i.e. I was no longer asked to be a leader.... Then I found a thin slice of a trunk of a tree with its 'ever-widening circles'. Nature speaks to me.

I call the kererū, the New Zealand wood pigeon, my Spirit bird because every time I see it, I recognise God is with me. (See photo section.)

On reflection, I recognise what a very varied and amazing life I have lived and most of it has been in response to a strong sense of call on my life. God's calls have come to me in very different ways; sometimes in a dream, but for most of them I have a deep sense within me that God is saying, "Marg, this is what I want you to do." Frequently this is the call that has come from beyond me, often with somebody or a group saying, "Marg, we have chosen you for this job, please will you do it?" And to my surprise I have said, "Okay," – because I have a deep sense that you God, are in this.

God, I prayed this morning asking you, "I need you to tell me what to write. I have no idea where to start. It's the season of creation. Richard Rohr has written beautiful stuff. And and as I'm sitting in my home watching the Kererū outside, and as I have lots of questions, I have decided to write about my relationship with you God, in the midst of creation. In the following pages, my story unfolds.

1 – Marg's Call[1]

I've been wooed by a few in my time, but none so exciting, so sensitive, so subtle, so attuned to who I am, as my God! I often go through my life quite unaware of this persistent wooing, but when I stop, take note, and abandon myself to this love – life changes.

This lover of mine, (and of yours), sends me gifts in so many ways. "Hey! Look how much I love you," (the call says), as I stand in awe of the sunset. "Hey, listen to this it's important," as I unpack my dreams or wake frightened with a nightmare. "Hey, I care for you," as my friend listens to me and holds me close.

Sometimes this wooing changes the outer structures of my life. Other times it has a profound effect on how I see myself and others, enabling me to sink even more deeply into this love that will not let me go.

As children, our family life was very simple. There was no talk of God, or spirituality. Nor was there any sense that my parents were against people who were religious; it was just an unspoken conversation. I was just turning five when my little friend said, "If you come to my Sunday School on your birthday, they'll sit you in the birthday seat, give you a birthday cake and sing happy birthday to you." What five-year-old would say 'No' to that? I went along and they did all that, and it didn't matter that the birthday cake was made of plasticine because I found a community of care. I kept going to the Methodist Church in Croxton, in Melbourne, almost every Sunday and later I went to the youth group. I found there the God who loves me so dearly.

Thirteen years later when Billy Graham came to Melbourne, I went with the youth group to hear him speak. I recall I was very unsure of him, but when he spoke, I discovered Jesus really wanted to be my friend and I needed to give my life to him. Later, I can distinctly remember walking up Ballantyne Street, where I lived, and sensing God's presence.

At Easter Camp I did just that. Aged 19, I was baptised. This experience changed everything as I saw everything was alive with the light of God.

About 20 years later, when the charismatic movement was in full force, I was resistant, but I was also aware people's lives were radically changing. Finally, I said to God, "OK, I want you more." The sense of mystery deepened when I discovered Spiritual Growth Ministries and its wonderful contemplative approach to life. I learned to dance with the Trinity (Perichoresis!): the One who is forever the friend, comforter and guide, mother and father, womb.

As I look back, I recognise God's been active in calling me towards very different forms of ministry. These calls have come in two different ways. The most amazing were sudden and surprising, changing my whole sense of self, of who I am and where my life was going. Then there are times when I just know that I know – that I know.

Call for me is a still small voice that speaks to me often as I walk the beach, do the garden or sit in spiritual direction. Sometimes it occurs in a dream, other times it's a deep sense within me. Frequently the call has come from beyond me, for example, from an individual or a group who have said, "Marg, we have chosen you for this job, please will you do it?" To my surprise I have agreed because I had a sense that God was saying, "This is what I want you to do Marg."

An example of a life changing call was when I was sitting in a Summer School happily expecting to continue teaching until the right man came along. Suddenly, I just knew I wanted to become a Deaconess. The notion took me by surprise, and I discussed it with Jack Goodluck, my Minister at Bentleigh Methodist Church who said, "Good. My wife and I wondered when you would hear the call. We must go down to Melbourne on Monday as the committee are meeting to finalise the arrangements for those going into college next month."

A mere five weeks later I was in college undertaking the requisite training, without having gone through all the hoops everyone else had to go through. I was able to give my school the four weeks' notice it required.

Similarly, life changing was the call to marry Warren Schrader and move from Australia to New Zealand. Warren was a widower raising seven children. His first wife Nan had died giving birth to their twins, then aged two. People, including my poor mother, tried to point out how difficult this move might be, but I knew it was the right thing to do. I went from being a single woman, the Chaplain of the Methodist Ladies College in Launceston, Tasmania, to being married to Warren, the Chaplain of Saint Andrews College in Christchurch, New Zealand, and the mother of seven children.

Several more amazing examples of God's wooing come to mind. There was the call of God to the ordained ministry of the Presbyterian Church Aotearoa New Zealand (PCANZ). I was surprised that the Presbyterian Church immediately accepted me. Assembly had just decided that those of their women who had trained as deaconesses and wished to be ordained into the Ministry of the Word and Sacrament, could be accepted without further training. While this was good for me, I still had six children at home, and I found this ministry difficult as I had not been trained in sacramental ministry. Fortunately, I had an excellent role model in my husband and the parish was a wonderful community where I could grow my skills.

Many years later, I was sitting in Assembly watching the second woman Moderator of the PCANZ, Margaret Reed Martin lead communion, when that still small voice I know so well whispered, "You'll be doing that one day." My response this time was, "Don't look, don't tell, and don't even think about it." I didn't think I was ready to undertake this role. At the time I didn't even tell Warren about this call. Five years later I'd been asked to lead a workshop at another Assembly, at which people from all over the church came up to me and said, "You need to be our Moderator." I hope I wasn't rude, but deep inside me I remembered that voice and I knew the time would come. I became Moderator of PCANZ in 1995.

The still, small voice spoke to me again when I was on a 30-day retreat, when instinctively I felt this deep sense that Warren was going to die. I sobbed for about three days until my Spiritual Director said, "We have no idea whether this is really about Warren's death or a metaphor in your life." Even so, without saying anything to Warren I began to take note when he sorted out the money and changed the washers and found myself being so much more attentive to his needs than I had previously been. Twelve months later when the doctor began to talk about him dying, I knew, and I was prepared – I'd done so much preliminary grieving. It wasn't easy but I was so grateful to our loving God who prepared me for this. Warren was only 63 and I was 50.

In 1991, I received the call to establish The Still Point as an ecumenical house of prayer offering, "spiritual direction, counselling, prayer, and massage therapy." Together with two Catholic sisters, Judith Anne O'Sullivan and Yvonne Munro, our team members all followed calls. We visited many Presbyteries around the country, and facilitated numerous workshops.

Another call came to sell The Still Point, the house of prayer, which was my home after Warren had died. Sitting in an Association of Christian Spiritual Directors (ASCD) conference in Christchurch, I began to sob when I heard the call. I told my friend, "I have to sell The Still Point and move to the beach." Obediently, I moved to Waikanae in 2004.

Then there was the call to my life as a Pastoral Minister with L'Arche, a community of people with and without intellectual disabilities. It was a wonderful, deep learning experience for me. And there was the call on my life away from busyness to stillness. Upfrontness to hiddenness. Less involvement with a lot of people – to being more with God – and more prayer. The call to retire and embark on a new spiritual direction. My life's journey has brought with it a real desire to go deeper with an openness to different approaches to body, soul, and spirit.

I've explored the 'Spirit in Nature' and see the way God's spirit permeates all things. The most obvious is my love of the Kererū, my spirit bird. I became conscious of this at my first retreat at the Buddhist Retreat Centre in Wangapeka, where my son Mark and his wife Kath were deeply involved and became teachers. A flock of Kererū kept flying past me every time I had a sense that God was with me. On the final day, we were gathered in a circle, when suddenly, a Kererū flew past, and everybody said, "Marg, look at your spirit bird." Since then, I've frequently sensed its presence.

In 2010, I went on a month-long Buddhist retreat focusing on dreams. I truly believe that God is in everything, so if I'm going to discover more about God, I need to follow the call even when it takes me out of my comfort zone.

In recent years I experienced a very strong call to interfaith ministries. I set up the first group meeting for 27 people from many different faiths in 2021. And now the call to write my story, hence this book. I've been hesitant about this, but I just know, that I know – that I must do this.

God's unmistakeable call doesn't just belong to the realm of the Bible. God has a habit of making sudden and surprising interventions in life. These are just some examples of call for me. Life is not totally under control, in fact not really under our control at all in any lasting sense. Faith for me is a combination of knowing that God is faithful, as well as a deep sense of my body saying, "this is the way to go."

The process of call goes on. Where to, I don't know, but I'm very sure it's the one I know as Mother, Father, midwife, womb, friend and mysterious one, lover and prodder, who knows me so well that I can abandon myself, knowing that the small voice, that speaks to me often, is the one who comes to me disguised as my life.

2 – My Mum and Dad

"Stories have to be told or they die, and when they die, we can't remember who we are or why we're here."

Sue Monk Kidd, from 'The Secret Life of Bees' page 107

My dad's name was George Moncrieff Stirling, and he was born in Amphitheatre in Victoria to a solo mum in 1900. His father married his mother in 1903 and then left her again very soon after that.

My grandmother gave my dad to an aunt who was a Tartar, a term used to refer to anyone who originated from the vast Central and Northern Asian region then known as the Tartary. The aunt, then transferred him to another aunt. My grandmother then got a job to earn money to keep him, but she died on his 13th birthday in Tasmania. Why do I start with all that when I've only just learned about it, and when there is so much else to tell about dad?

Was dad a very strong man emotionally or was he closed down? I often asked him to tell me about his childhood and his parents, but he'd always say, "You don't want to know!" Many years later, when I went home to Australia to see him after a huge heart attack that we thought would kill him, he recovered and insisted to the rest of the family that he would drive me to back to the airport. So, speeding along the three-lane highway to Tullamarine Airport, and with us in the right-hand lane with all the signposts showing 'Airport left lane,' I who'd never argued with my father, was holding my breath and my seat when he said, "Marg you always wanted to know about my father, now it's time to tell you!" I grabbed an envelope out of my bag and listened and wrote. I've lost the envelope and I was so scared we were going to crash that I can't remember anything he told me. Luckily, I've since found out something about him.

In 1974, dad sent me a book in 1974 called, *Gang Ahoy – A Stirling Notebook*, it traces our line back to 1130! There were Stirlings in three places in Scotland including the Keir Stirlings. Would you believe one of our boys is Keir – not a very common name. One lovely bit about the Presbyterian Stirlings I learned was that they were converted to Methodism by John Wesley. The thing that amazes me is that our history is full of clergy and doctors – my brother and nephew became doctors, and there were musicians. The names that kept appearing are the same names of our little nuclear family – Elizabeth, George, Margaret, and Dorothy. I discovered that there was in Melbourne a Robert Stirling prize for students of surgery. Later, my brother George introduced open heart surgery to Australia. There was also the Isabel Jesse Stirling who was awarded a prize for nurses. A little unexpected, I learned of a Stirling Fashion Centre in Richmond, where Dame Nellie Melba used to shop. George Stirling the owner, installed the first store Tea Room so people driving in from the outer suburbs could stop for tea. Later, my son Paul opened a restaurant in Wellington. And would you believe a George Stirling, around the end of 1900, introduced golf to Victoria and founded the Melbourne Golf Club! My dad was a brilliant golfer and played most weekends.

When I read all this, I was enraged as I had a sense of growing up with a very empty background. No grandparents, uncles, aunties, or cousins, and yet there's this amazing history and all these fascinating people that I knew nothing about. I began to ask myself, "Who am I? Did my dad know this, and if so, why did he not tell us?" Then my rage changed. I became angry at the unknown Stirlings, who must have known that we were there.

After a few walks along the beach processing what I had learned, I realised that Grandpa Stirling was probably the black sheep of the family. The family may never have known that he produced a son. I also realised that belonging to an 'important family' had its downside and I didn't have to cope with that growing up.

Did dad try to contact them? I do not know and probably will never know. The important thing for me is that I discovered a very rich heritage and a deeper understanding of my dad. Anything I held against him, has been forgiven, and I know I am better rounded person because of it.

"If you want to understand any woman you must first ask her about her mother and then listen carefully. Stories about food show a strong connection. Wistful silences demonstrate unfinished business. The more a daughter knows the details of her mother's life, without flinching or whining – the stronger the daughter."

Anita Daimant, from 'The Red Tent,' page 4

My mother was a woman of her time. Born in England in 1898, she had no siblings, no aunts, no uncles. She was raised as an Anglican came to the new land of Australia by boat when she was 13-years-old with a woman I knew as 'Aunty Ruby'. She was a woman of her time, and culture – very British, quiet, and well dressed.

I know very little about mum and her nuclear family, but I do have my memories of her and dad and will share them with you in the following pages.

3 – My Early Life

I was born on the 2nd of February 1939 in Melbourne, Australia. The youngest of three children, I was an unexpected addition to the family when my mum Dorothy Stirling was 41 years of age, and my father George was 38. In my prayer recently I was suddenly struck with a deep sense of knowing that I was probably unwanted. My sister Joan was 13 years older than me, and my brother George 11, so having a new baby sister in the house must have been a surprise to them too. I imagine a new baby was the last thing they wanted.

Growing up I recall our family life was simple, quiet, and stable. My parents' roles in the household were traditional. My dad was the breadwinner in the family, and mum, who had been an only child herself, was the homemaker. Like many of the Stirlings, dad was a teacher. He was a self-made man, putting himself through university. An avid reader, his speciality was English literature, and he wrote a book on English grammar. At the pinnacle of his career, he became the principal of Brighton High School in Melbourne, then the largest secondary school in Victoria. He was also the Chair of the Headmaster's Association. In his spare time, I recall he was a keen golfer and often came home to say, "I got a hole in one today," as he put yet another beer mug on the mantlepiece. No one in our family drank beer! We just said, "Ah ha," not understanding the significance of it. Later dad taught me how to swing a golf club in the back yard, and how to putt on the rolled lawns. He was also a keen member of the Masonic Lodge and became Master.

Dad was a kind and gentle man. He showed little emotion, neither happiness, joy, anger nor sadness. I was always aware that I was deeply cared for and felt safe at home but was never sure if I was loved. Unlike my friends who received lots of hugs, kisses, and words of affection, in our home there were no verbal or physical signs of affection except when I kissed my mother and father on the cheek as I left the house and when I went to bed. Looking back, I realise that my very strong need to be good and not cause a fuss came from that.

There was a rhythm to our lives. Dad always came home from work at the same time and was very dependable. When I came home from school or sport, mum would be at the table, waiting for me, drinking a cup of tea, and reading her book. There would usually be a companionable silence as I got myself a drink and sat with her. She was an excellent housekeeper, and a good cook; there were always good hot meals at the right time – 6pm! Mum was also a keen gardener, and a skilled dressmaker. I was never asked to sweep a floor or use a vacuum cleaner, and I certainly did not learn to cook. Mum would often say, "Marg, get out of the kitchen. Do your schoolwork, that is more important." I think she was happy to do it all because it filled her day and everyone else in the family were busy doing important things. Mum always made sure we were well fed and watered, and when my parents hosted card parties for Dad's friends, she was an excellent hostess.

I think mum was a couturier dressmaker before her marriage – but that might have been a rumour. We'd go shopping together to purchase the material for my new dresses and she made all my clothes. The photo of me in the beautiful Tea Towel dress (made by my mum) is the only photo I have of us together until my wedding. (See photo section)

One of the things I feel sad about is that I didn't ask her to make my wedding dress. I was living in Tasmania at the time and came home a few days before the wedding. She never shared her disappointment, but I read it in her face.

As my siblings were so much older than me, and following their own direction in life, my memories of mealtimes were that they were very quiet. That is until my teenage brother George found his voice and argued with dad! Shock horror – no one argued with dad! Later, when George became the Head Prefect at Melbourne High School, he was awarded a scholarship at the Royal Military College, Duntroon in Canberra. When he came home and broke the news mum was in tears and dad put his foot down shouting, "You are not going to Duntroon. You are going to university and be a doctor." George did as he was told and went on to study medicine. Clearly it was the right career path for George as he studied medicine, became a very successful surgeon, and subsequently introduced open heart surgery into Australia. George married Shirley, who was a nurse at the hospital, and they had five beautiful children.

Many years later, I took a boyfriend home who said, "I could never marry into a family like this, you are all so quiet!" It wasn't a demonstrative family. Mum was an extremely quiet, introverted, self-possessed woman. I don't remember having deep discussion with my mum or dad about feelings, things happening at school, spirituality, or sex. In fact, apart from the Duntroon discussion, I only remember seeing mum cry a few times. On these occasions she would suddenly start sobbing at the dinner table, then get up and go to the bedroom. Dad would say, "humph," and I would go to my bedroom and wonder if there would be a divorce. Things were always back to 'normal' by breakfast the next day.

Someone once told me that my mother was a beautiful singer – I was amazed to hear this. I can recall that we used to have people around for carols, where I think mum played the piano – but this memory is a little hazy. Mum was a member of the Alfred Hospital auxiliary and took on the role as President one year. She also played Crazy Whist but as she was a private person, I don't recall anyone 'popping in' for a chat.

As a youngster I attended preschool and was friendly with Shirley Palmer who lived nearby. In 1944, turning five, I went to Thornbury Primary School.

Although our home was full of books, I don't remember ever talking about them. My reading consisted of Enid Blyton and Biggles. It was only later when I heard from those my dad had taught, how he had engendered a wonderful love of English literature, that I realised what I had missed out on. Dad was deaf and wore one of those old-fashioned hearing aids. When my friends came, he would sit and talk to them for a few minutes and then I would see his hand slide into his inner coat pocket, and I knew he had turned off the sound.

We didn't go to church and although there was no talk of God or spirituality in our home, I was allowed to attend Sunday School with the friend who invited me when I was five years. When I told mum and dad of my first conversion – my baptism into the family of God at the age of 19, their response was, "OK." In this process I discovered a community of people who cared for me, loved me, and began to nurture me in the faith. This sense of family has never left me. Many years later I learned that my mother was an Anglican and my father had been a Methodist lay preacher – but this was never discussed.

On leaving Thornbury Primary School I spent two years at North Fitzroy Central School.

I remember when dad bought a tape recorder for Brighton High School. He bought it home with him and unbeknown to us, he had hidden it in the dining room. When he got mum talking, it was fascinating to me as she spoke in a way that I had never heard her talk before. When dad played it back to us, it showed that mum had lots to say when she was called forth, and then I realised he was just showing off his new toy.

In my teens I attended University High School (1952-1955) where I passed the Matriculation Examination of the University of Melbourne. I enjoyed all aspects of school, and was very keen on sport, particularly hockey. In my final year at High School, I became Head Prefect, just as my father and brother had been at the boy's school. For some strange reason, we had a church service and I had to read Isaiah 55. Dad had me practice it over and over. I can still recite it out of the Authorised Version today, "Ho everyone that thirsteth, come ye to the waters…."

As Head Prefect I had to give an end of year speech to the students and their parents at the Melbourne Town Hall. Dad coached me through this assignment. It was he who helped me to prepare and present my speech and I am so grateful to him, as these skills have stood me in good stead throughout my life.

Every year, during the school holidays, mum dad and I spent three weeks at Ocean Grove Beach in Geelong. As Joan and George were so much older than I, few of these were spent together. Dad and I loved the beach. Mum sat on the sand reading all day with her fair English skin. I suspect she hated it, but she never complained.

While on vacation, dad taught me to swim, float on my back and to surf, while mum spent her time sitting on the beach reading or watching us swim. I remember dad would go beyond the waves and float on his back for ages, and we would watch from the beach. Every now and then mum would ask, "Is your father still breathing?" I would say, "Yes," and she would continue reading. Each night mum and dad would play scrabble together.

Whilst mum and dad encouraged us to do our best at school, it was assumed that both my sister Joan and I would become teachers as, "This is what the women in the Stirling family did." We didn't question this decision – it was taken for granted that we would follow this career path, and we did.

Joan became a Physical Education teacher and taught at Murrayville School in Mildura. One of my best memories of Joan was probably when I was about eight or nine when I spent a week's holiday with her in Murrayville. We had a lovely time and Joan took me to the dump where I found a very pretty cup and saucer. At the time she was engaged to Dugald and we went swimming. One day, we were in the ladies dressing room shed, and he was next door in the men's when I heard him singing, "The girl that I marry will have to be, as sweet and as pink as a nursery. The girl I call my own will have buckles and braces and smell of cologne." I clearly remember thinking, in the wisdom of my youth, "that's not my sister, it's not who Joan is," but of course kept my mouth closed. Not long after that, they broke off their engagement. Joan married Bill Palmer whom she had grown up with. He lived across the road from us, and they had known each other since they were three. It was a very comfortable match, and soon after they moved to another suburb and started a family. Joan taught Physical Education at Bendigo Teachers College for a while. I remember being very proud of her when the Queen came to Australia as Joan was one of the teachers that organised the display on the Melbourne Cricket Ground.

Following my graduation from High School I enrolled in the two-year teachers training course at Melbourne Teachers College (1956-1957). I remember that my parents were immensely proud when I graduated.

It was while I was attending teachers' college that I became very involved with the youth group at Croxton Methodist Church. I felt a real sense of belonging to this community.

4 – Teaching Years

My teaching career began in Melbourne in 1958. In Term 1, I taught at Eastmoor Primary School in Bentleigh, and I went on to teach at Keon Park Primary School in Preston.

I was teaching at Keon Park School the year the Australian government allowed four-and-a-half-year-olds to start school. Unfortunately, they hadn't done anything about providing us with extra rooms. I clearly recall I was teaching with 56 five-year-olds at one end of a church hall, while another woman was teaching 44 four-and-a-half-year-olds down the other end of the hall. On reflection I'm fascinated at how well we did.

As a young teacher I became actively involved in the Bentleigh Methodist Church. There I discovered a community of people who cared for me, loved me, and began to nurture me in the faith. This sense of family has never left me. When the Minister offered baptism, I readily accepted the call. I was baptised into the family of God at Easter Camp when was 19 years old. I remember telling mum and dad that I had become a Christian and she said, "That's nice dear." I wanted to talk to them about some of the important things going on in my life, but there was usually a very short response.

I took part in all the Easter and Summer Camp programmes. One year, a few weeks before going to the Methodist Summer School, I had gone out with Denham Grierson, a minister who was going to give a talk about men for the ministry and women for the Deaconess Order at the event. I recall he said, "I hope we get lots of men but pray that we don't get any women. A terrible job!" To explain, the Methodist Order of Deaconesses was established to provide opportunities and a professional pathway to women in the life of the church. Recognising women had a place in the ordained ministry, it offered structure, support, and status for women in the ministry, both at home and abroad.

I said, "I'm coming to Summer School, but there is no way I am going to become a Deaconess!"

I went to Summer Camp, and as I listened to my friend speak, my whole body was suffused with a deep sense of knowing that I wanted to become a Deaconess and needed to apply. The notion took me by surprise. I discussed it with Jack Goodluck, my Minister at Bentleigh Methodist Church who said, "Good. My wife and I wondered when you would hear the call. We must go down to Melbourne on Monday as the committee are meeting to finalise the arrangements for those going into college next month."

When I shared my sense of God calling me to be a Deaconess with my parents, my mum said, "Oh! What's that?" I had to explain what a Deaconess was. When I had finished mum said, "I know what I'll do, I'll buy you some sheets and towels to take with you." The poor souls must have been a bit worried. I later learned that dad had been a lay preacher and mum had once been a devout Anglican. Goodness knows where all that went.

Six weeks later, without having gone through all the hoops everyone else had to go through, I gave my school the four weeks' notice it required, and I was in Esperanza. I had discovered, to my delight, that I'd finished my years of apprenticeship as a teacher.

I began training as a Methodist Deaconess in 1962. We studied at Esperanza, (a Spanish word that means Place of Hope), in Kew, an inner suburb of Melbourne. This was located next to the college for men wanting to train as clergy. I remember discovering that we, the women, were going to get a diploma after two years training, while the men would receive a bachelor's degree which would take them five years. Nevertheless, we had classes together and that was good.

I enjoyed college. I particularly enjoyed having two good women as my colleagues – Ruth and Merle. As I get older, I'm even more aware how open and liberal those who taught us were at the time. Many years later, when I was sitting at the feet of a woman theologian in the USA, she mentioned something about woman in the gospels. Over afternoon tea, I said, "That's what Rev Harris told us." She enquired as to which university I heard this and was surprised to hear that the Rev Harris was just a local Methodist minister down the road from Esperanza, and the minister of the local Methodist Church.

As part of the two-year Deaconess training course, students were required to undertake work experience in the community during the holidays. I worked at Epworth Hospital in Melbourne. This was an on-the-job opportunity to learn about life and death.

I was ordained in Wesley Church in Melbourne on the 14th of October 1965. The service was conducted by the Rev R.J. Philip, President of the Conference, and the Rev C. Gallacher, Ex-President, delivered the Charge. My two years' training and three years' probation gained me a Diploma of Religious Education, whereas the men I trained with had five years training and gained a Bachelor of Arts or a Bachelor of Divinity. Mum and Dad attended the ceremony and were immensely proud of me.

Ruth and Merle became engaged that year and sadly, in accordance with the rules of the day, they were unable to be ordained.

After my ordination I was sent to the Methodist Ladies College in Launceston, Tasmania. Given my teachers training, as well as the theological training I became their chaplain. Initially I felt a bit overwhelmed with the responsibility, but there was good support.

5 – Meeting to Marriage

I'd been working at the Methodist Ladies College in Launceston, Tasmania for two years, where I lived in the boarding house with the girls. I took prayer each day during assembly and did a lot of counselling. Fortunately, someone suggested I get some training and so I joined the Marriage Guidance Group.

One day, I heard that D.T. Niles, a theologian from Sri Lanka, was going to be in Perth. I really wanted to meet him and hear him speak, but given the distance (nearly 3,000 kms), I couldn't afford the travel expenses this would incur. I approached Megan Cootes, the Christian Education Officer for Tasmania, to discuss the matter. Grinning she said, "Yes, but he's also going to be in Hamilton." This was great news as Hamilton is a small town, north of Melbourne, close to where my family lived. As I filled out the relevant form, I wondered why anyone would go to Perth when Hamilton would be more readily accessible, when Megan said, "D.T. Niles will be in Hamilton, New Zealand, not Hamilton in Australia." In response I said, "I'm going there then aren't I," and she replied, "Yes, it looks like it." Unable to fund a trip to Perth, I found the money to travel to Hamilton in New Zealand.

Together with Helen Cook, the House Mistress at Methodist Ladies College, we travelled to New Zealand in 1965 for the event and planned to explore parts of the North and South Islands over the Christmas holidays. Arriving at the Hamilton school where the event was to be held, I vividly remember being met by a gentleman who said, "Marg Stirling? You are the leader of the Australian party aren't you?" I told him he was mistaken, nevertheless he said, "Well, your name is on the list, would you please go and sit on the stage for the welcome." Following the instructions, I headed for the stage and sat next to a nice gentleman who suggested, "Let's swap seats, there's about to be a Māori welcome. I've seen them before, and you won't be able see much from here because of the man with the big Greek orthodox hat on." So, we swapped seats and then he introduced himself, "My name is Warren Schrader."

After D.T. Niles' presentation, Warren, and his colleague Ron O'Grady, the General Secretary of the Conference, offered to take Helen and me to see the sites, and this gave us the opportunity get to know each other. I learned that Warren was a Presbyterian minister, the chaplain of Saint Andrews College, Christchurch. We talked a lot about what we did at our respective schools, and discussed how we talked about resurrection with third formers, and what we did about incarnation with sixth formers etc., etc. I enjoyed the company, and the conversation was immensely interesting. We also discovered we had so much in common. I listened while Warren chatted happily about his seven children, but he never mentioned his wife, so on the last day I asked him about her. He said, "She died two years ago giving birth to our twins, so I'm bringing the children up." This was interesting as I had thought he was a happily married man.

Towards the end of the Conference, Alan Brash, the Head of the National Council of Churches, spoke about the 'Freedom from Hunger Campaign.' During his presentation I began to sense that God was calling me to give up my luxury holiday, find work and give the money to the campaign. When I told Helen about my experience, she laughed, breathed a big sigh of relief, and said, "God's been telling me the same thing. We need to get jobs and give the money to the poor." We discussed the experience with Warren who fortuitously found us both a job at Woodchester Retirement Village in Christchurch.

Time sped by and all too soon the Conference concluded. Before going our separate ways, Warren invited me to meet his children while they were on holiday at their beach house in Paraparaumu, and with that we said our farewells to one another.

Accompanied by Napi Waaka, Helen and I set off on a trip around the East Cape to learn more about Māoritanga, and then went on to explore other parts of the of the North Island. Arriving in Paraparaumu, we spent a day and a night with Warren and his children at their beach house. Apart from meeting the family, my two abiding memories are the first earthquake I had ever felt, and the next day when Warren and his seven children, who ranged in age from 13 to two, took us down to the beach. There was Warren with a shovel over his shoulder to build a fort and the kids dancing along the waterfront in a long line dancing along the waterfront singing, "Oh Ho, Oh Ho, it's off to work we go." We had lots of fun.

Leaving Paraparaumu, Helen and I headed to the South Island to undertake our holiday jobs at Woodchester Retirement Village. While in Christchurch, Warren invited us to have supper with the Schrader family. All too soon, our vacation came to an end and both Helen and I returned to the Methodist Ladies College in Tasmania for Term 1 in 1966.

The Letters

When I arrived back at school, the first letter from Warren was there waiting for me. I knew before I opened it that I would marry him. I recall the moment. It was the first time I had even thought about loving him, and I certainly didn't know what that might mean.

In the first letter Warren asked simple questions like, "Tell me what the 10 most important thing about you are. What you'd really like to do in life? What you hate etc…"

I responded, "Goodness, you do ask difficult questions and if I answered them like that it would sound very stilted. Let's just get to know each other as we write about our lives."

There began an amazing correspondence where we discovered so much about each other and how similar we were in outlook, theology, ideas about child rearing, music, literature, how we took Christian education classes, what we did in chapel with the kids, about our family backgrounds, and how this was still affecting us. And of course, I heard a lot from Warren about his beloved children and the complications of trying to find someone to care for them while he worked.

We were both using *Come out of the Wilderness* – James Baldwin's story of race relations in the United States and Ruel Howe's book *Man's Need and God's Action* with our classes. This was a far cry from the set curriculum, but met the students' needs in a very exciting way. Sometimes I received four or five letters a week from Warren, and one of these was 18 pages long! Through these letters we experienced a meeting of minds. Warren confessed that he would have loved to have held me in New Zealand, but was too afraid to do so at the time.

I am not sure that I had any such feelings. For me at first the attraction was a meeting of minds and a shared set of common interests.

Many of Warren's letters were written very late at night, after he had put the children to bed and prepared classes for the next day. I was surprised that nobody picked up the fact that something special was happening in both our lives and even commented on all the letters crossing the Tasman. The other thing that surprised me as I re-read our letters was that in mid-February, I was the first to suggest he come to Australia in the May school holidays. He had planned to go to Fiji for a church meeting but decided that I was more important!

I was also the first to broach the subject as to whether this relationship was to be permanent and whether we would marry! What a forward young woman.

I realise now that Warren was probably very aware of what marrying him meant, while I was blithely unaware or certainly not willing to look at it. The school counsellor, Molly Campbell Smith, who shared a room with me, asked me several times whether I had thought through the ramifications of marrying a man 13 years older than me with seven children. Molly reminded me that I had changed the subject each time, and I am glad because I would hate to have been frightened off by practicalities.

After much to and froing we decided that it would be best for us to meet somewhere other than with my family and decided on Sydney. Warren made the arrangements. Re-reading these letters I began to see some of our differences. For example, I am very frugal, and Warren was not. He was captivated by the thought of buying gifts from the Duty-Free Shop.

We met at Sydney Airport and wanting to look my best I had my hair set. We hired a car and I clearly remember he drove into a lay-by and kissed me. We had a great time getting to know one another. It was obvious to us both that we were well suited and would get married. I wanted a proper proposal, and we decided that the Sydney Harbour Bridge was the most romantic place. We drove up there one wonderfully sunny day and to our horror discovered it was the busiest, noisiest, smelliest place one could imagine. Hastily changing our minds, we drove down to the beach at Manly where Warren proposed to me in grand style.

Warren and I continued to correspond with one another until the day we married. The children also wrote to me, and I to them. Unfortunately, it's not possible to include all their letters here, but you can see their personalities shining through. (See photo section)

I've kept all our letters, including those from the children; they weigh 2.45 kilograms and stack close to 16 centimetres in height. What a treasure.

I wrote to my parents to tell them I was in love with Warren, a New Zealander, who, oh dear, was 13 years older than me! And help, he happened to have seven kids. Dad wrote back straight away saying, "It was inevitable that something like this would happen to one so full of life. It seems natural that you should be drawn to one in a similar calling. We have always trusted you to make good decisions. Whatever you do you can rest assured that you will have the full backing of your mother and me. Naturally we look forward to seeing you both at Easter."

Mum also wrote back, clearly bewildered by the news, "How on earth will you manage a ready-made family of seven, plus I hope, a few of your own? And then there is the housework." And then she listed all the things I probably did not know how to do from nappy changing to cooking meals – and she was right, I didn't know how to do these tasks. She went on to say, "I have such great faith in your own good sense. I am trying to persuade myself that all things will turn out well in the end. Whatever you do we shall be right behind you. It's much easier to write this than say it because I'm afraid I would dissolve into tears."

I guess I wrote back saying, "Don't worry mum, it will be OK." This could have been a wonderful conversation but it's one we didn't have.

I remember taking Warren home to meet my parents. He won mum over by asking her if he could make her a wee cup of tea.

On hearing the news of our engagement, Warren's mother wrote to me, "Welcome to the Schrader family! It was such a thrill to get the phone call last night with such exciting news and I know the other members of the family join me in wishing you both lots of happiness."

It was clear that Warren's mother looking forward to meeting Marg and embracing her into their family.

Colleagues

Within a few months I shared the news of my intention to get married with colleagues and friends in the Order. Helen Cook, who was with me in New Zealand when we met Warren and his children, was overjoyed on hearing our news and looked forward to visiting the family after the wedding. The decision was made official when Warren and I became engaged, and this meant that after two and a half years, I had to resign from my role in the Methodist Deaconess Order. Shortly after, I began the process of handing over my responsibilities at the Methodist Ladies College in Launceston, Tasmania and tidying my business and family matters in Australia. Fellow staff members at the Methodist Ladies College arranged several farewell celebrations within the community, and the wives of the Methodist ministers organised a party for me before I left the role.

At the time the transition from my previous life as a teacher, deaconess, and chaplain of a Ladies College in Tasmania, to being a young wife and mother of seven children in New Zealand, seemed quite daunting. It was a significant change in direction, away from everything I had known and experienced to date, and I was totally unprepared for the role of wife and mother. Although apprehensive, I knew it was the right decision. I'd received the life changing call to marry Warren Schrader and move from Australia to New Zealand and I looked forward to it.

The Wedding

I remember going out to the airport to meet the five older children, Jan, Jon, Kay, Keir and Mark and Nanny, Warren's mother and Auntie Shirley, Warren's sister, neither of whom I'd met before. The twins who were only aged two, remained in New Zealand cared for by their Auntie Anne, Warren's other sister. Jan, then aged 13 got off the plane in a beautiful blue suit she had made herself, with the most amazing white boots she bought on 'appro'!

The night before I married Warren, I was washing the dishes when dad came in and said, "Humph. Margaret, I have something I need to say to you!"

"Yes dad."

"You know a car ran over you when you were two and a half years old, the doctor said you may not be able to have children normally. Thought you needed to know."

"Thanks dad, I have been to the doctor and had it fixed."

End of my sex education lesson!

The following day, Tuesday, the 23rd of August 1966, Warren and I were married at West Bentleigh Methodist Church in Melbourne, and I received as a gift his seven children. *The Sound of Music* had just hit the screens! Life was not quite as romantic as that for us. My good friend, Jan McDermott, was the senior bridesmaid and Jan, and Kay Schrader were the junior ones, all dressed in orange velvet.

Jan, my friend had the flu and looked and felt terrible. During the service conducted by the Rev Frank Morris, Kay fainted, and my brother George came to the rescue and said, "It's alright, I'm a doctor," and promptly managed the situation. The service resumed when Warren suggested we sing the next hymn.

My strong memory is that Warren and I slept in the house with the children on our wedding day. Jon, then aged 11, came into the bedroom to say goodnight and with a wicked smile on his face said, "Have fun mum and dad!"

The next day I took the children for a walk while Warren packed up their cases. Mark saw a matchbox car in a shop window and asked if I would buy it for him. I said, "Sorry, Mark I don't have any money on me." Jon said, "Don't you remember she said she gave all her worldly wealth to dad at the service!"

'All my worldly wealth I thee endow'!

When the children returned home to New Zealand, Warren and I spent a few days in Melbourne with the family, then took off to Queensland for a short honeymoon before joining the family in Christchurch to begin our married life together.

6 – Married with Children

Family

Transitioning from my role as a chaplain to being a mother and a housewife in New Zealand, was a steep learning curve; one I embraced whole heartedly. The children ranged in age from 13 to two-year-old twins. Jan the eldest was 13 years old, followed by Jon, Kay, Keir, Mark and the twins, Tom and Ben who were then aged two.

All of the children responded to my coming in very different ways and all with very different needs. I cannot imagine how hard it was for them, losing their mother and then having to accept this new person in this important role in their lives. They too had to learn the different ways she had of doing things. It certainly wasn't a bed of roses for any of us, and at times it was very hard. I am so grateful to each of them. My own mother was always dependable and trustworthy. I wanted to be this kind of a mother too and show the children that they were loved.

I vividly remember waking up in my new family home in Christchurch. I could hear the children pottering around, so I got up and said, "I'll go and help with the breakfast." Jon was in the kitchen, and I asked him what the family usually ate for breakfast, and he said, "Porridge and bacon and eggs. You make the porridge and I'll do the bacon and eggs." I had never eaten porridge and had no idea how to make it. I expected it to be in a packet with directions, but no, it was in a huge glass container, with no instructions! I gave it a go, and luckily it turned out alright – there were no complaints! Years later, when I was telling Jan the story she said, "We never had all that for breakfast, we could never afford it!" Jon was having me on, and I'd been caught out! Oh, I'd so much to learn and we were going to have lots of fun along the way. When I think of this it takes me back to my mum in the kitchen saying, "Marg, you go and do your homework, that's more important than trying to learn how to cook and clean." If only we'd both known.

Although Warren and I had been doing very similar work, neither of us thought of the possibility that we might share his job and share the tasks of home and family life. No, he continued to work as a chaplain, and I ran the house and looked after the children. It would be very different today.

With the financial constraints of a minister's salary, and many others like energy and space, Warren and I both knew that we could only have one child together. This child was to be the most loved and wanted, and I expected it to be a girl because we already had five boys and only two girls. We decided not to wait too long so the baby could easily fit in with the rest of the family.

I reckon I know the time I conceived. Mary Rose, an American working for the Parish Development and Mission Department (PDM) offered to 'babysit' all our children in Paraparaumu. The Oranges of Khandallah, who were friends of the family, loaned us their house, so Warren and I had a weekend all to ourselves without any nappies to change or kids to organise.

My strongest memory of that weekend was returning home and seeing all the kids looking so happy and well cared for, and the twins' nappies sitting firmly on their little bottoms! Mary Rose had fed them 'Smores' (marshmallows dipped in chocolate – an American treat).

As Nan, Warren's first wife had died just two and half years before while giving birth to Tom and Ben, I was given the very best attention. Dr Vivien Croxford, the best obstetrician, and the only one in Christchurch who allowed fathers into the birthing room was my obstetrician. The only hospital at the time that allowed men in was the Bethany, the Salvation Army Home for Unmarried Mothers. Vivien suggested a physiotherapist who taught me how to breathe and other womanly mysteries. Vivien reassuringly advised that as I was so busy, and hence fit, I was very well prepared for the birth and commented that I had no time to be anxious.

On the morning of the 5th of October 1967, my due date, I visited Vivien who assured me that the baby was still a while a way. I went home and did some gardening, but then felt quite ill. We rang the doctor who said it must be a tummy bug, so we got on with life for a few hours until my waters broke. We rang Ann, Warren's sister, who came immediately to babysit, and we rushed to the hospital. Four hours later, our family expanded with the arrival of our son, Paul, at 10pm. What a lovely little boy!

It was a delight to be able to stay in bed, have my baby brought to me and have nothing to do for 10 days except enjoy the little bundle. During those days a nurse asked all the new mums if they wanted to learn how to bath a baby. When I asked if I could join in, she said, "Oh I thought you had lots of experience!" Anxious that I couldn't feed the baby all he needed, Paul had to be bottle and breast fed. Vivien said with a laugh, "Just sit down and read a book for an hour before each feed time!"

On the day I was due to be discharged from the hospital, Warren arrived looking very concerned and announced, "the twins have measles." Consulting with the Matron we were advised to go home and contact our local GP. A locum, who didn't know us came to the house, looked at all the other children and said, "Well you know what to do, you have lots of experience." When we explained the situation he grunted and said, "Well all you need to do is put the twins in one room, and the baby in another. Change your clothes as you go from one room to another." As a very scared, inexperienced, young mum, I did exactly that!

Paul was a beautiful gift to our family, and I made a very strong decision never to favour him in any way. I was very grateful that he woke most mornings about 3am and I was able to offer him all my love in words and cuddles as well as milk. While bringing up eight children was difficult, and exhausting, it was also a blessing. It was the most important and hardest job, but the most satisfying role of all.

We lived in Christchurch for four years, during which time life was incredibly busy as a mum and a minister's wife.

In May 1970, when Paul was only three years old, my mother died and was cremated in Springvale Botanical Cemetery in Victoria, Australia.

My mother was a woman of her time, and she did the very best she could. She was dependable, trustworthy, and never complained. I always knew my mother would be there for me and our home was safe. As a young mum I hoped that some of these qualities rubbed off on me too. I was always concerned about my mothering skills and my relationship with each of our children and I wanted to ensure that they all knew that they were loved.

Wadestown Presbyterian Parish

Again, in response to a call from the Wadestown parish, Warren was appointed the minister for Wadestown Presbyterian Church. By this time, Jan, the oldest of the children was attending university, and chose to remain in Christchurch. We packed everything up and the rest of the family travelled by ferry to Wellington. The trip was easy enough apart from the twins being sick on the ferry all the way down my front.

Arriving in Wadestown the parishioners were a very welcoming and caring community. As a young mum they embraced me and cared for me and my children. I have very happy memories of the years we spent there. The first Sunday I remember sitting with the children as Warren took the service. We sat next to Elizabeth Purdie and her children; I thought, 'this is a family a bit like ours I want to get to know them.' I looked around the church and felt immediately at home. I later discovered that Elizabeth had set up and ran Open Home, a midweek group for people who needed friendship and companionship.

Roger and Heather Lane were another couple who were deeply involved, as were Phyllis and Bruce Purdie. The thing that I really treasured about Wadestown was the wonderful sense of community, and the ability to see people with very different understandings and experiences of God as one body. I remember Roger Lane was so good with the young people and ran the Christian Youth Movement.

Frequently, whenever we talked about something good happening in the Parish, classic little things like somebody visiting somebody sick, or somebody taking someone to hospital, it was often the charismatic members of our parish that were doing this. It was as though something very special happened to them. I was aware that I didn't have that same sense of life and vitality that many of them had.

I loved the Wadestown Parish. They had great interest in caring for people, including the elderly and the sick, and an interest in justice issues. Two of the great stalwarts of the parish were Keith McEwen and Ethel Curtis.

As our children became more independent, I worked in the parish providing as much Christian education and pastoral work as other commitments allowed. It wasn't all smooth sailing raising seven children, and one of my own. In effect we raised eight teenagers in a row – that's desolation at times. But life wouldn't be as rich if there wasn't desolation. My relationships with these kids wouldn't have been as strong if we hadn't gone through a bit of hell. The painful bits make me who I am. I'd be a simpering woman if everything was sunshine in my life.

When Jon our oldest boy was diagnosed schizophrenic, it wasn't an easy time. When he was at school, I had been frequently told how bright he was. I vividly remember the day Warren and I went to collect him from the Porirua Mental Hospital. The specialist told us that Jon would no longer be able to hold down a job and needed to give up university. We queried this advice and when Jon was told, he very clearly refused to believe it. He went to university and studying under Professor Lloyd Geering, he nearly completed an MA in Theology.

Although tired – always exhausted, I did my best, but in those days, I sometimes struggled with prayer. It was the beginning of the charismatic movement, and I was initially resistant as my theology was more liberal than I thought theirs was. For example, members of the church were divided when it came to the Gay community – there were issues around them being accepted in the church. This hurt me deeply, I yearned for inclusion, it's a big deal for me. I knew I had to change how I shared my perspective on the wider issue with our community and asked for God's help.

One day I rang up Ainslie McDowell, one of the leaders of the charismatic group, and said, "Ainslie will you pray with me?" She said, "I'd love to Marg but we're just about to go away on holiday." I sighed with relief, and then about two minutes later she rang and said, "Bob has said if Marg Schrader wants to pray, we will do it now!" So, I went. I was very aware that my desire was for something of the life, they said people had, but I didn't want to speak in tongues, and I didn't want to raise my hands, and I didn't want to have those frilly bits. But then Ainslie and Bob began to pray with me, and my heart and my whole body was filled with so much life and vitality. I found myself lifting my hands and speaking in tongues. Praying with Ainslie McDowell I had a transformational experience – a sense of bodily weight being lifted off me, of electricity coursing through my body. God became very real, and my prayer life changed completely. Later, as I walked down the street, I had the sense of the whole of life becoming more vibrant as if the spirit was present in me and in all of life. Thank you, God.

After that I became much more contemplative. Sitting still and very quiet I would experience the spirit. I knew it was a real gift, and I'd done nothing to 'earn it.' I loved it and it opened me to God in a whole new way. I trust that if I allow myself to be open, then God will meet me.

While working in Tasmania, I had shared an office with a Counsellor and with her assistance I too trained as a Marriage Guidance Counsellor. The training was invaluable. I was able to apply these skills many times over both in Australia and in New Zealand. In 1977, in response to a call, I became the co-director of the Wellington Marriage Guidance Council. Through Wendy Cockburn, my co-director, I was introduced to the Transcendental Meditation (TM) technique, and began a daily mediation practice, which I found hugely beneficial.

Although life was incredibly busy, by the late 1970s our youngest Paul, was 12 years old, and I increasingly recognised my own call to ordained ministry. Bruce Purdie was very encouraging, and I was surprised that the Presbyterian Church immediately accepted me. Assembly had decided that those of their women who had trained as deaconesses and wished to be ordained into the ministry of Word and Sacrament, could be accepted without further training. I was relieved about this, as I still had six children at home. Warren was most supportive, and a wonderful teacher. I was ordained in 1979 and inducted as an honorary assistant minister in the Wadestown parish, joining my husband Warren in a 'team ministry.' I was thrilled that my father came to my ordination.

Warren and I became one of a small group of three 'clerical couples' in the Presbyterian Church. I initially found the role difficult as I had not been trained in sacramental ministry. Fortunately, I had an excellent role model in my husband, and the parish that we shared was a wonderful community in which to grow my skills. With their support I could really see myself working in parish development and encouraging the congregation to strengthen the things they were already good at. Seeing the Church as a caring community, I continued to work in marriage guidance, marriage enrichment, supporting and strengthening families, and mission development.

The Pacific School of Religion

In 1984, Warren and I went on study leave to the Pacific School of Religion. While there, I went to a course on feminist theology facilitated by Rosemary Radford Reuther, a leading biblical scholar who was also exploring the lost feminine side of God in the scriptures. We were asked what our sense of God was. As I was in a strange land, and no one knew me I said, "womb." She answered, "biblical," and then moved on to the next person. At the time I was too shy to question her. Later, I discovered a book by Phyllis Tribble called *God and the rhetoric of sexuality*. In this book Tribble spoke of the Hebrew word for compassion *Rachamin* (Rechem) – which has the same root as the word for womb. Many times, in the first testament the word compassion could be translated, "God's womb trembles." I bet every mother knows what that feels like!

On our return to Wadestown, we had a family camp at Forest Lakes. I was longing to speak of God's womb – but didn't. I was too afraid of how people would react! It took a long time for my confidence in using feminine images of God to settle, and even then, it was more likely to be expressed in terms like 'mother' and 'midwife.' But now I am confident as I know I am safely enclosed in God's womb.

Parish Exchange to Levittown, Long Island

That same year, Warren and I were offered a parish exchange to Levittown in Long Island. Paul, being the youngest and still at school, came with us and went to the local school. Tom and Ben also joined us for a short time.

New York is the most amazing city. I know why people get enchanted with it and want to keep returning to it. There were so many things to do, sights to see, experiences to have, varieties of food to eat and people to meet. The variety of prepackaged food was mind boggling not to mention the number of fast-food outlets – there were at least 10 of these within a mile of our home and some of them were 'Drive Ins' – another new experience for us!

When Ben was with us, we took to the freeways, which was a bit of a mission at first, but we quickly developed our confidence to get to and from the places we wanted to go. With Ben we spent our days visiting art galleries and museums and had a good look around the United Nations building.

The parish was very beautiful. When we arrived, it was covered in snow. Warren and I planned to work part-time while we were in the United States, and the people were open, caring and very accepting of all we had to offer. We attended numerous committee meetings and soon became familiar with how the structure of the church worked in the parish. The feedback from the parishioners was very encouraging and I felt as though we had arrived in the right place at the right time. I ran a Spiritual Growth Group and facilitated a 'Healing of Memories' course. Warren became involved with the WCC programme and took part in the 'Images of Life' study. Within a short space of time, a delightful nun, Sister Sadie Nessor, offered to become my Spiritual Director.

I attended a course facilitated by Walter and June Wink in Pennsylvania on 'Discerning the Will of God' and was thrilled to have the opportunity to attend another course called 'Dreams and Images – Personal and Biblical' – something I'd always wanted to do.

During the 15 years we lived and worked in Wadestown, the children had all grown up, left home, and were exploring their own paths in life. When the call came again to move to Palmerston North in 1985 to be part of the Parish Development and Mission Department (PDM), it took quite a bit of discernment. This was new territory for both of us. As consultants for the Churches from New Plymouth to the Wairarapa, we were to work with the parishes to help them deepen their relationship with God, explore their mission, and help with conflict resolution.

By this time, we had collected an enormous amount of junk – I realised I had married a hoarder! In the garage I heard Warren say to the man who was assessing how much space we needed in the moving van, "I will have cleaned out all this before you return." Of course, he didn't. I was in the garage again when the removal van came, and I heard the man say, "I think we're going to need another van," which of course we did.

7 – Move to the Manawatu

We moved to Palmerston in 1985 to take up our roles with the Parish Development and Mission Department (PDMD) Team, and Paul, our youngest child came with us. Lester Reid was the excellent leader of this team, whose members were a very gifted and diverse group.

Our service in this area allowed a much wider group to benefit from Warren's special talents, and it gave me the opportunity to develop my passion for spiritual growth. Together and independently, we affirmed the worth of the anxious and encouraged people to explore new dimensions of ministry. I led workshops on prayer and was part of the early years of Spiritual Growth Ministries and assisted at St Albans in Palmerston North. It was a very demanding job with lots of travelling and we met so many new people, but God constantly reminded me of his faithfulness.

Meanwhile, I became involved with the Retreat movement, first through the Cenacle Sisters, and then through our own Spiritual Growth Ministries. This was an important move for me as God drew me in deeper. Warren and I enjoyed a very stable, comfortable, and supportive marriage. By this time, we were proud grandparents to several grandchildren, and while Warren was looking forward to retiring, I planned to continue to work 'alone' – yet not alone.

My most common form of prayer is to 'just sit' and be at one with God. I used to be very verbal and active, but I didn't seem to have the energy or the desire for that in the mid to late 1980s. I used the daily lectionary readings as my base and dreams became an important means through which I believe God speaks – so I always do a lot of work on them.

Over the 1987-88 Christmas and New Year period, I attended a 30-day Ignatian Retreat at Mount St Mary's in Hawkes Bay. It was the first time I could consider leaving my family for that length of time and I was excited and scared about the 30 days of 'Intense Prayer.' I had heard stories of how the experience had been for some, but for me, 30 days of silence seemed at this point in the year to be sheer bliss. Thirty days of Spiritual Direction is a real gift. I was being called more and more into Retreat work with very little formal training and while this wasn't the aim of the exercise, I wanted to be open to what God wanted me to do.

On the Retreat, we prayed through the life story of Jesus and how it affects our life. While there, I suddenly sensed that Warren was going to die. Stunned, I sobbed for about three days. When I shared my experience with Clare, my Spiritual Director, she said, "We have no idea whether this is really about Warren's death, or a metaphor for your life." Reflecting on her words, I integrated that thought and went on with the retreat – going deeper into the story of Jesus' life.

While on the retreat, Warren wrote to me, sending his love, sharing his thoughts and activities, and as always, offering encouragement and support.

> "I am enjoying pottering around and you'll see fruits of that when you come home… I miss you. It's you not anyone else that fills that hole. Because of all we've been through, and still do, I rejoice in your expanding, reaching out, risking, following your own star even more beautiful Marg… who, wonder of wonders, is the wife of Warren – friend, lover, partner, neither subjugated or dominating, leading sometimes yes – why not? Moving to a zenith (because that is where you are in life – so why not?) With things to teach me… and I too still with things to share with you." And signing off, "Go well… love you (even in absentia). God continue to bless you."

Warren's letters are a treasure, I still have them.

Almost exactly a year later, Warren was diagnosed with acute myeloid leukemia. We were told he did not have long to live. I knew then that my sense of deep intuition experienced at the retreat, and on other occasions, was real. Over the previous 12 months I had taken great care to watch Warren as he changed light bulbs, fixed leaking taps, and sorted the finances. I had often wondered how he juggled the money so that we didn't go without anything we really needed. I had also been much more sensitive to his needs. My love for him grew. When the diagnosis came, Warren was shocked – but I wasn't.

Those first few weeks were very difficult. Warren kept on talking about, "when this is over, we could go overseas." He said, "I need this operation to remove my spleen, why don't you go and do the study leave we were going to do together, and I will fly over when I'm finished." You can imagine how I felt about that.

Finally, Warren woke up one day and said, "I am going to die aren't I?" What a relief as we were then able to talk about it at such great depth. It was one of those very special times. I'd done so much preliminary grieving. It wasn't easy but I was so grateful to our loving God who prepared me for this. Warren wrote an amazing letter to his friends and our children started to come together from all over the world. Warren would talk to them, one at a time to conserve his energy. This very quiet man, usually so introverted would say, "What do you want to know about me?" The children, who as adults had spread their wings, all came from around the world to be with us, to say their 'thank yous' their 'sorrys' and their 'goodbyes.' It was a very precious time for all of us as they could ask all those questions that they'd never asked before, and then come back to the rest of us and share it all. I was overwhelmed with the richness and beauty of the family we shared and their love for him, for each other, and for me.

Warren took great delight in preparing his funeral, choosing hymns and scripture readings, and saying who was to do what. It was sometimes quite funny. Shirley Murray wrote a special one for him called, 'When human voices cannot sing' (*Alleluia Aotearoa* 151). Although we were grieving terribly, we were well prepared for the inevitable. Warren died within three months of the diagnosis in 1989. I clearly remember the night he died. The nurse was there for the first time. When she sent me to bed she said, "I'll call you when you need to be here." Halfway through the night she called us as Warren was nearly ready to go and we all told him how much we loved him, and he just smiled his last.

I was only 50 when Warren died. We had been happily married and worked in partnership for 23 years. Although we certainly had our share of ups and downs, Warren was a loyal, loving, gentle, patient, and sensitive companion. We had a shared love of ministry. He encouraged me to be me, but was not afraid to criticise when he felt it was necessary. He was one of the real male feminists. He saw my potential and encouraged me to develop it – theologically, churchwise and with the family. He supported me, even pushed me to do the things he knew I could do, even if I was doubtful. Thank you, Warren. Thank you, God. Amen.

To celebrate Warren's life, one of his friends compiled many of the letters we received. Here are some examples of the memories they shared with us. Donald Feist from Dunedin said,

> "There was always an openness and directness about Warren – in a gentle and thoughtful, not a harsh or noisy way, that I felt challenged me to a similar integrity in return. His real concern wasn't for a controversial issue but for the people most involved. I think that was typical for the people who were being overlooked or undervalued and not understood by others. His voice in Assembly was a voice of thoughtfulness and sanity."

> "Warren at Otago was always the effervescent centre of a bubbling circle of students – usually brewing a good stir about some social question… I was struck by Warren's resilient spirit, crusading zeal and infectious enthusiasm, still coupled with sensitive feeling for the 'less fortunate' or the 'underrated,' or the 'put upon.'" *Samuel McCay, Howick*

Hearing the news of Warren's death, my niece Jill, and her husband Len Firth, who also shared a ministry, wrote from Australia,

> "I have always been encouraged by your marriage and the way you were able to work together in ministry. It is a rare achievement in my experience. It was a joy to see you accepting each other and allowing each other to be yourselves and enjoying each other so much. I am glad to have been able to have shared in your life together, it has given me a lot."

Warren's obituary shone a light on his life's work:

> "An outstanding pastor and perceptive counsellor, Warren brought to worship a freshness and warmth that was his own distinctive natural style. To his work he brought a willingness to learn and a recognition of what was valuable. Innovative and positive. His encouragement drew fresh efforts from others and his common sense appealed to lay and clergy alike."

The children and many others spoke at Warren's funeral.

Before the service we listened to some of his favourite music:

- *Jesu Joy of Man's Desiring* – Jacques Loussier Trio
- *We will All Remember Paul* – Dave Brubeck Quartet
- *Send in the Clowns* – Benny Goodman
- *Veni Santus Spiritus* – Taizé Community
- *Sicilienne* – Jacques Loussier Trio, and
- 'Passion Chorale and Chorus' – *St Matthew Passion*, J.S. Bach

Although we were heartbroken, the time of Warren's dying was a real gift to us all. While we ached with the pain of not having him around, the weeks preceding his death were filled with healing love, new life, and deepened relationships. Family and friends were thankful for the prayers, love and practical support we received, and for the gifts given to Spiritual Growth Ministries. We were supported in ways beyond anything we could have imagined.

Warren's Poems

Warren wrote poetry. His poems are a treasure. The selection included in this chapter are my favourites.

Lilies in the Field

You really are extravagant God –
my flower is the epitome of beauty … form … texture.

Soft in colour
A core of intricate simplicity
Yet you made thousands upon thousands of these
     which as you say last but a day
     before going into the oven.

And you make thousands upon thousands
     – different varieties
     – different sizes
     – different colours

What a waste
     utter waste
     no use at all

But then that's not your purpose in creation, is it?

You make us in your own image
     to be You in your world
     Your partner

So, you surround us with signs of your constant loving tenderness
     ever extravagant
     ever loving
     always more than we deserve
     or can cope with

Truly you are a gracious generous God
     and you invite me to be as generous and as gracious
     equally with you to respect your creation
     equally with you to enjoy your creation
     Thanks God

p.s. – I like daisies too

[Oct 12 4.30pm]

Suddenly

Shafts of piercing sunlight invade my bedroom
announcing the gift of another day of life
in a world of myriad wonders

Light
Life
You – the giver of life and light
and that brilliance I stand again amazed

5 minutes later dense clouds bury that sunlight
Rain falls gently on an already soaked earth –
another sign of your utter liberality
no discrimination
no apartheid for you
whether black or white
guilty or innocent

You send your rain on the just and unjust
Just as you pour forth your love
in the pregnant bud on the grape vine
the soft bowl in the head of a brilliant tulip
in the trusting eyes of a baby
or in the comforting unfolding arms of a best friend.

Gifts all
with no strings attached

But an invitation
('love one another as I have loved you')
Gratias deo – for all these wondrous gifts of grace
Gratias deo – for your love that I can give to others
and receive from others
Gratias deo – for your initiating love that sparks my love
so day by day the wonders of life
continue to enfold

Wonder
upon wonder
upon wonder

[Oct 12 AM]

Prisons!

What are these for you Warren you ask.

You know – as I know
Some of them we share

With Paul I see myself **intending** one thing
       and **doing** another

I see myself promising one thing
       and never getting around to it

I see tradition determining action
       stubborn self will – as determined as that process
       in a factory mass producing:
       once begun it continues on
       so inexorably
       until the final product emerges
       A lack of discipline on myself
       procrastinations too

Prisons!
       implying I am bound
       bound by something outside myself
       when in truth I imprison myself
       I hand over the keys
       and sometimes the lock has not been turned
       (as Houdini discovered)

I just think
       assume
       I am locked in
       when I just have to push the door
       and step into freedom

Bread – and wine

Gifts of bare earth
  cultivated
  watered
  by human hands

Gifts of the Son
  broken, as was his body
  red as was his blood
  poured out
  in a death
  from a world he so loved,
  for a world he so loved.

I come and stand by you beloved sister in Christ

Beside you as you dip into your catholic cup
  and I break my bread
  drink my wine
  from my protestant source

I wondered whether to leave you standing alone…
  that in your exposed loneliness
  we could all see
  why Marg weeps tears at your Mass

That
  would have spoken much – powerfully
  your utter loneliness
  before Christ's Table
  who intends to make us one
  and whose gifts of bread and wine
  are neither catholic or protestant
  Yet not alone before that Cross

For the one who gives us life
  gives us bread and wine through the Son
  breathes his presence amongst us, into us;
  still wondering – surely – at what we've divided

A death, and gifts, before that death meant to make us at – one

Yet still we break that life apart
        and strangely too we draw closer together

So as a sign of hope
        as a sign of wanting to be together
        I came out
        I stood beside you

In reality
        we took different bread and wine
        – or so it seemed

But in a deeper sense of that same reality
        we were brother and sister in Christ
        deo gratias
        gratias indeed

[Oct 12 AM]

In the aftermath of Warren's death, Mark returned to Canada, Keir to Perth, Kay to Oamaru, Tom to Auckland, and Jan, Jon, Ben, and Paul to Wellington.

Later, I took the opportunity to take two months study leave and left for the Church of the Saviour in Washington D.C.

8 – The Still Point

When I returned from study leave in July 1989, I chose to remain in Palmerston North, and continued my work in spiritual direction with the Presbyterian Parish Mission and Development Team. Following Warren's death there was a period of adjustment. By this time the children had all left home and were pursuing their own careers, interests, and some of them had families of their own.

Two years later I resigned from my roles with the Parish Development and Mission Department Team, and St Alban's. I felt I needed to do something with our big, six-bedroomed home in Albert Street in Palmerston North. Trusting the process that all would become clear in due course, I sensed the call to use our home as a place of prayer – a place where people could come for stillness, spiritual direction, retreat, and workshops. I discussed the idea with friends John and Trish Franklin who were very supportive and then I went on a retreat with Judith Anne O'Sullivan OP, a Catholic nun. When I explained what was happening with my vision, she exclaimed, "I'm coming too," and I excitedly agreed! Together, in 1992, we established our house of prayer and named it – The Still Point from T.S. Eliot's *Christ is The Still Point of the turning world*. My daughter-in-law, Mary Daish, is an architect. With her guidance and expertise we refurbished a couple of the bedrooms making one a prayer room and the other for Yvonne Munro's massage therapy and counselling. Later Mary transformed the garage into another room to meet our needs.

Family and friends came together to plant bulbs and ferns in the garden – a symbol of new life.

I've always encouraged others to develop their inner experience of God and find new ways to share this collectively in worship. My approach to worship has been influenced through the charismatic movement, contemplative prayer, and ongoing investment in my own spiritual growth. The people I've been privileged to meet along the way who have also influenced my learning journey.

I wanted to develop alternatives to traditional, intellectual, formal modes of worship and connect with people who long for worship that leads them into God's presence. I also wanted to provide silent, contemplative prayerful spaces and encourage creativity to help them make connections between everyday life and faith. Using fresh images of God, and contemplative spiritual styles can be an effective and significant form of outreach, to touch the lives of many who are interested in spirituality, but are put off by religion. The Still Point certainly became a place of stillness and growth for many people. I am so grateful to God for this experience. The Still Point was such a beautiful place to live and work in.

The inspiration and ideas for The Still Point were informed by my own spiritual journey. There were many such experiences.

One of these was the Spiritual Guidance Programme I attended in the early 1990s at the Shalem Institute for Spiritual Formation in Washington D.C. It was here that I met Gerald May, my supervisor for my thesis, *The Effect of Sexual Abuse on Women's Naming and Experiencing of God*. The Shalem Institute draws on the wisdom of a broad variety of religious traditions and provides resources for contemplative living, prayerful readings, retreats, and programmes for clergy seeking to go deeper. It was a wonderful opportunity to participate in the Contemplative Prayer Groups. Understanding first-hand the value of these experiences, I was keen to share all I'd learned with our community when I returned home to New Zealand.

While in Washington D.C., I visited Christ House – the first 24-hour residential care facility for the homeless with acute medical needs in the Unites States. This facility offers comprehensive and compassionate care and a broad array of services and activities for their patients to help break the cycle of homelessness. The day I visited the facility, I distinctly recall looking at the statue that stands in the forecourt of the building. There was a homeless man sitting nearby, and it looked to me as if he was having a very deep conversation with the statue. I said, "Tell me about him." Without hesitation he said, "It's Jesus – he was homeless too. He really understands what I am going through."

I attended numerous retreats both in New Zealand and offshore. This included a Shamanic workshop in the Marlborough Sounds, and a Silent Retreat at the Pastoral Centre in Palmerston North. In addition, I spent time at Four Springs in California, a sanctuary located in woodland, miles from anywhere, that offers retreats and seminars that integrate religious wisdom and psychology. I attended in-depth seminars on The Synoptic Gospels, and a few years later, returned to immerse myself in the Wisdom Literature of the Hebrew and Christian Scriptures.

Through these experiences, and the experiences of Judith Anne and Yvonne, we developed a distinctive ministry at The Still Point. This included innovative worship known as a Sacred Space where we introduced people to contemplative prayer. I'd been pregnant with the vision for this for many years. It was like a baby growing within me. It was a vision for worship that is Christ centred and contemplative. This worship style takes seriously the words of the psalmist, "Be still and know that I am God," and the words of Jesus, "Come apart with me to a quiet place."

This worship at its core, had a time of silence, where people could meet God in the depths of their own hearts. The worship involved all who were present, was not hierarchical, and had no one up front telling everyone where to sit or stand, or what to think or believe. Our worship took everyone's personal journey very seriously and enabled people to be free to express their faith, doubts, love, and fears. Our worship seriously acknowledged that we are very sensate people with strong imaginations, and that we all find God in very different ways.

When I talked about this vision, I discovered a wonderful group of people who were longing for the same thing, and not only that, but they were also sensing a call to be part of its formation and leadership. Eleven of us formed a group that prepared the worship, and we were overwhelmed at the response. We encouraged people to pray in silence with their senses, their imagination, with clay and with dance. This was very popular and large numbers of people joined together each evening. It was fun, deep, incredibly satisfying, and very inclusive. This experience was real soul food for me, and I was grateful for the wonderful ecumenical group to work with.

We were delighted when Yvonne Munro, a Josephite Sister, joined us in 1995 as a Counsellor and offered massage therapy. We also offered retreats, supervision, spiritual direction, particularly for women, and dreamwork.

I'm also so grateful to have shared this experience with Judith Anne and Yvonne, the two amazing women I worked, played, and prayed with.

Reflecting on the experience Judith Anne said,

> "For me the important dimension was we were Ecumenical and lived very much from the Word of God and prayer. We also knew how to care for each other and how to play and celebrate to keep a balanced way of life. The women who came for prayer, support, spiritual guidance and whatever else was needed, became an integral part of our life and we were not just there to do a job but more importantly to become the people God was calling us to be. To be honest, although I lived in a Community of Dominican Sisters at the time, The Still Point Community was just as important and a very significant part of my journey to life in God. Marg who owned the property was extremely generous in making it feel we all held ownership. Our life together at The Still Point was aptly named as the sacred space was indeed a Still Point, a place for nourishment, affirmation, and challenge."

The following passage resonates with me, sadly, I cannot remember who the author is. I've included it in my memoir as it has special significance.

The Still Point

> In the stillness, the movement of God can be seen.
> As we slow, the acceleration of His work within us takes place.
> When we cease, the very heartbeat of God can be felt.
> We are able to reach out and touch His reality,
> Experience His union.
> Delight in His company and He in ours.
> In the quiet, we hear the sounds of our struggles,
> The cause of our fears,
> And meet with the One who washes our tears with His own:
> Jesus, our Stillpoint.
> As we pause from our every-increasing circles,
> Our true path is revealed with clarity.

The unnecessary weight of our load is realised
And we set out again with a free and still spirit.
'Be still…and know…that I am God.'

(Psalm 46:10)

Studying and promoting feminist theology, I drew on Sophia Wisdom – the female metaphors and wisdom of God, personified as a woman in the scriptures. This resonated with me. The word that most aptly describes my relationship with God is 'womb.' I feel as though I'm surrounded by God, fed, and nurtured. God's love fills me. I've also worked consistently to create safe places for women to explore their spirituality in ways that are most appropriate to them, with a particular calling to work with people who are struggling with the Church as an institution.

To illustrate, I'll share a small sample of my favourite metaphors of God, quotes from the scriptures, and Bridget Meehan's poem entitled *Who are your God?*

Sophia: Woman of Justice

Scripture Image

With me are riches and honor, lasting wealth, and justice.

(Proverbs 8.18)

God: A Midwife

Scripture Image

Yet you drew me out of the womb, you entrusted me to my mother's breasts, placed me on your lap from your birth, from my mother's womb you have been my God.

(Psalm 22:9-10)

Wisdom: Playful Craftswoman

Scripture Image

When God set the heavens in place, I was present,
When God drew a ring on the surface of the deep,
When God fixed fast the wells of the deep,
When God assigned the sea and its limits – and the waters will not invade the land

When God established the foundations of the earth,
I was by God's side, a master craftswoman,
Delighting God day by day ever at play by God's side,
At play everywhere in God's domain, delighting to be with the
children of humanity.

(Proverbs 8:27-31)

God Who Gave Birth to Humanity

Scripture Image

You were unmindful of the Rock that begot you,
You forgot the God who gave you birth.

(Deuteronomy 32:18)

The Mother

As a mother comforts her child, so will I comfort you; and you will
be comforted in Jerusalem.

(Isaiah 66:13)

Who Are You, God?

I am the womb of mystery
I am the birther of new life
I am the breast of unending delight
I am the passionate embrace of a woman
I am the emanation of feminine beauty
I am the Mother of Creation
I am the cosmic dance of Sophia Wisdom
I am the sister of courage, justice and peace
I am the feminine face of God you have longed to kiss.

Bridget Meehan, Exploring the Feminine Face of God!

Retreats

Judith Anne recalls,

"We were often invited to conduct retreats or workshops from The
Still Point and I remember people used to say to me, 'You said such
and such with great Wisdom,' and I knew it didn't matter whether I
had said it or the Wisdom came from Marg, or Yvonne. Provided the
Wisdom was received, what did it matter whose mouth and heart it

53

came from. We were certainly not competitive. Our desire was that Jesus, our first love, be shared with all those who consciously, or unconsciously longed for Him."

Judith Anne and I, along with Presbyterian minister John Franklin, were invited by a bishop to run the priest's retreat. I asked the bishop, "What about Eucharist?" He paled and said, "Oh, I haven't thought of that. I've got into a lot of flak for inviting you. I'll go home and pray and let you know tomorrow." He came the next morning looking worried and said, "I am sorry. I'm unable to say, 'yes' to you." I felt deeply for him and understood some of the pressures. For me, interfaith recognises and welcomes the spirit of understanding of all faiths in the love of God.

Regardless, the retreat went ahead as planned. As I sat in the back row during Eucharist, I began to sob. Later, at dinner, one of the priests asked, "Are you OK? I saw you crying." I answered something like, "I find it painful not to be able to eat with the family." He gulped and said, "I've never thought of it like that." There were many more retreats of this nature, and each time I wasn't permitted to receive communion. This was significant part of my spiritual journey.

In 1995, following a call, I was chosen to be the next Moderator with the Presbyterian Church. One of my aims was to help people re-discover God and get in touch with their own deep longings. My hope was, and still is, that they would be open to the surprises of God, who calls us to love each other and to listen to each other at depth. The Moderator role and function was complimentary with our work at The Still Point, and I'll share more about this experience later. While undertaking the Moderator role, Judith Anne or Yvonne often travelled with me to Presbyteries around the country and helped to facilitate the workshops. It was interesting to take them into rather conservative areas such as Southland. There were times when the male Moderators took their wives for support, so this was unusual, as my companions were catholic Sisters. But once Judith Anne and Yvonne offered their gifts of prayer and deep knowledge of God and humanity, they were welcomed with open arms. Judith Anne recalls this being one of the highlights,

"When Marg was elected as Moderator for the Presbyterian Church, she invited Yvonne and myself to companion her on various missions.

I think that said it all, as we were indeed one in the Mission of The Still Point focussed on the healing and growth of all those who longed to live a deep spiritual life."

Throughout these years The Still Point community met and helped so many people, from all walks of life, including those who had been sexually abused. Many women entrusted me with their stories, and they all affected me deeply. As I had trained as a sexual abuse counsellor, I was able to integrate spirituality and counselling at The Still Point. We all grew through the experience, and I'll share more about this topic and the strategies that have helped me in this work later.

We also enjoyed family times at The Still Point. I recall the Christmas of 1997, when 18 us gathered there. We had a wonderful time, and it was so good to see how well the family get on together.

In 1998, Judith Anne received the call to change direction and take up a new position with the Aquinas Institute in Missouri for six months. I understood and supported the call but knew I would miss her badly. We had started The Still Point together and had been such good friends throughout the process. Reflecting on the experience Judith Anne said,

"Even today I look back on my time at The Still Point with deep gratitude to God and to Marg who so believed in being inclusive. She was more than willing to share her dream with whoever God called to it. It was a very formative time for me, and I am grateful for the wonderful women who inspired me and trusted us to be a significant part of their healing. I think my motto at that time was 'With God all things are possible' – and they sure were. Many thanks dear Marg."

Yvonne and I were sad to lose Judith Anne but understood her call and wished her well on her spiritual journey.

It was time for Yvonne and me to revisit our original vision for the place and together we explored new possibilities for the future. Yvonne introduced the metaphor of the Clown Ministry. Yvonne expands on the concept,

"The Clown Ministry is definitely about the Christ. It can remind us of the joyfulness of life, a celebration. A clown elicits laughter. People naturally identify the clown with joy, celebration, laughter, victory over difficulties and playfulness. The clown is able to reflect these qualities."

Yvonne was a wonderful clown, who was able to demonstrate the many aspects of God, Jesus, and life. Initially people may have found this odd, but within minutes they could relate to the metaphor, and responded well to the concept.

Time passed and life continued at The Still Point and I attended various Assemblies and conferences. In 2003, while sitting in an ACSD conference in Christchurch, I began to sob. I had sensed the call to sell The Still Point, the house of prayer that we'd set up in my home after Warren died, and move to the beach.

Whilst it was a wrench, I followed the call.

I am grateful to God for The Still Point. It was an oasis for people to discern the Spirit of God at work in their lives. It was such a beautiful place to live and work, and I treasured the relationships I developed with Judith Anne and Yvonne – two amazing women to work, play and pray with. While together, the three of us enjoyed twice yearly wonderful holidays.

Leaving to continue our individual life journeys, we celebrated the life of The Still Point (1991-2003), and the people we had met and touched.

The closing words were:

> As we separate, and the ties unbind, and the threads of our lives disentangle, and we make ready for a new weaving, let us believe in our hearts:

- That nothing we have shared together that is good will be lost,

- That all we were takes its honoured place in our life's journey,

- That nothing is cancelled, but some things are settled and concluded, that there is much we cannot say or communicate none the less abides and endures,

- That nothing can separate us from your love, in your love.

> Amen.

Celebrating the life of
The Still Point
1991 – 2003
and the gifts of
Judith Anne O'Sullivan, 1991 – 1998
Yvonne Munro, 1994 – 2003
Margaret Schrader, 1991 – 2003

If a grain of wheat falls
on the ground and dies,
it yields a rich harvest

Celebrating the life of The Still Point

9 – Moderator's Memories

It happened twice. Both times at assembly. Once when Ian Cairns was Moderator in 1985, and the other time was when Margaret Reid Martin was in the chair. On both occasions, I had this deep sense of knowing that one day I would be a Moderator. I was stunned and horrified. So horrified that I did not even tell my husband. I pushed it as deep down as I could, and I did not even pray about it. Looking back, I can now say that deep sense of knowing came from God. It was to prepare me for a job that I did not want, and that was bigger than anything I ever thought I was capable of doing.

I realise now that I was also in front of the Assembly a few times. Once when working with Parish Development and Mission Department, I had a dream about how we all needed to be responsible for the state of the church, and not hand it up to the people on the stage. I shared my dream with the PDM staff, and somehow, I was asked to share it with the Assembly. During this period, I gathered as much information as I could about the communal discernment. Many were delighted and as usual, some were horrified.

I suggested that I was going to pray, "Lord, renew your church beginning with me." It caught on and someone printed it all onto the yellow stickers that we all wore, even when we went back to our parishes!

I recall, back in 1983, when Warren and I were Neil Churcher's chaplains, we supported him in every way we could. At that time, we were engaged in discussions about the very fraught Baptismal controversy. Oh, how we Presbyterians love to argue and believe that we have the whole truth.

A few years later, at another Assembly in 1993, also fraught with tension, I took worship and spoke of the very different ways we all experience and speak of God. That evening many people from right across the theological spectrum came up to me and said, "The church needs you." While protesting, I knew that the time was coming, and I needed to say my 'Yes.'

When the vote was taken, and I was facing the reality of the task, the women of the church gathered around in great numbers. In preparation, Joan Anderson, and Margaret Reid Martin, the two previous women Moderators, flew me up to Auckland to talk woman Moderator talk.

Pamela Tankersley, (who later became the fourth woman Moderator in 2006), organised a fund to clothe me. Three artists from Palmerston North – Betty Crawford, Natalie Watkin, and Vonnie Davis, gathered with me and designed and made stoles for my alb.

Esther Willis peeled potatoes with me in my kitchen and spoke of a wall hanging that she'd seen that was entitled, 'One Bread, One Body.' I said, "That will be my theme." She then made a very large wall hanging that many of the women's groups added to. We asked each parish to make a small banner expressing the theme. Once again, women from all over the country used their creative skills to beautify the Saint Andrews gym with these and powerfully expressed the unity of God's church.

Shirley Murray gifted us with a hymn about the theme, *One Bread One Body*. The Reverend Alison Ballantyne, chaplain of the college, painted huge murals to illustrate Jesus' parable of the woman who put yeast into a measure of flour.

The Assembly was held at St Andrew's College in Christchurch from 14th-19th May 1995, the college where Warren had been a Chaplain. Judith Anne and Yvonne accompanied me, and my family were there too. I am so grateful for their friendship, love, and support, and often wonder what I would have done without them.

On the 'big day,' Yvonne helped me dress for the Induction Service, and Tame Takao from the Māori Synod loaned me a beautiful cloak to wear.

One of the most powerful moments for me was when the past Moderators laid their hands on me to induct me. The choir of Saint Paul's in Christchurch led us in *Veni Sanctus Spiritus* (Come Holy Spirit), and the choirmaster had written verses in Māori, Samoan and Korean. Millie Te Kaawa and Keir Schrader read the scriptures, and we recited the *Moderational Servant Prayer*, written by I. Gore.

I chose the theme 'One Bread, One Body,' as we were experiencing enormous pain over the issue of homosexuals in ministry, and the church was divided and not trusting of each other. In keeping with the theme, during each of the subsequent business sessions, the women of Christchurch baked bread so that the aroma of the yeast rising, and the baking bread wafted through the Assembly. This was another of those tense and fraught Assemblies. I was able to stop the Assembly after one particularly painful time and asked the women to bring the steaming bread up to the table. I broke the bread, a symbol we often used, and using it as a metaphor said, "We are a broken body. Kyrie Eleison."

I spoke of the way Christ's body was being broken again and asking that people take the bread and do what they needed to do with it. Perhaps give it to someone they feared they'd hurt, or someone they wished to feed, or even sit in silence with God with their food for this journey.

I became Moderator when the church was going through a very difficult and stressful time of social unrest. My key task as a Moderator, was to address the divisiveness, referring to the theme 'One Bread One Body.' Many people described my role as the 'mother of the church.' I found that difficult. After all, I was not sure how good a mother I was with my family. Nevertheless, when the children bickered, I used my role as a mother to call the 'children' to look for common ground. I mention this because at one stage during the proceedings in Assembly, I stopped the debate and told them a story – it was when I had my eight children in the car, and they were arguing amongst themselves. I told them how I would stop the car and tell them to sort it out before I would start again. I explained it was not safe for me to drive with that noise in the back. I suggested we sit in silence and do what we all needed to do with God. It usually worked, although I frequently felt as though I was the mother to a wonderful family who sometimes got out of hand.

Then the work began...

Michael Thawley was the most amazing 'right hand man.' I could never have done the task without him and Paul Ranby.

Paul Ranby was the convener of my Moderator's committee who was a tower of strength and kept my feet on the ground.

The programme was scheduled as shown in the flier in the photographs section.

These fliers were distributed, along with the Moderator's Menu I had developed, whereby each of the Presbyteries could choose which workshops their community would like to engage in when I visited them. Through these workshops, using a family therapy model, I wanted to help people to rediscover God, get in touch with their own deep longing, and talk to each other about the issues that we faced. I also hoped that, during the dialogue, they would be open to listening to each other in depth.

Marg's Moderator's Menu

A. PASTORAL

1. One Bread, One Body

An opportunity to explore the theme from biblical, theological, and psychological perspectives. We look at creative ways of listening to others and living with differences. We will search for ways of praying with another's point of view and praying for healing of our inner wounds.

2. Women Stand Tall

A time to look at our lives in the light of the lives of women in the Bible. We talk, pray and play.

3. Journey In, Journey Out

An opportunity to listen for the call of God in our lives.

4. Stress and Spirituality

We will explore the ways in which stress affects us for good and ill. This will include not only the normal stressors but also the pain of our inner wounds. We will then find ways of praying and living in God's world that will help us to live life more abundantly.

5. Dreams, God's Forgotten Language

We will look at some of the numerous biblical stories of how God guided people through dreams. Then we will find ways of relating more clearly to God, others and ourselves through our own dreams.

6. Praying Our Goodbyes

For anyone experiencing loss of any kind. A chance to recognise, and reflect on, the variety of losses that are part of our everyday lives. We will learn from Jesus's prayer as he faced the losses in his life.

7. Highs and Lows – A Time for Families

Time for families to explore ways they can mark special points in their life together – births, deaths, coming and goings, achievements and redundancies, growths, and griefs. Suggest a meeting over a tea hour, 5.30-8pm Friday, or 4.30-7pm Saturday. Fish and chips for tea, or potluck.

8. Growing Old With God (for those 60 plus)

'For everything there is a season... a time to plant and a time to sow.' We will explore the season of your life and ways of deepening our relationship with God.

9. Switching Onto The Awesome God (for young people)

A chance to meet God personally through prayer, scripture, and silence, and each other.

B. PRAYER

1. Going Deeper

An opportunity for us to deepen our relationship with God by exploring some of the rich traditions of prayer in our Christian heritage.

2. Enabling Prayer in Others

For clergy and lay leaders – exploring the art of enabling others to pray.

3. When Darkness Descends

We will explore what happens and how to cope when prayer is dry, and God seems to have disappeared.

4. Exploring the Many Faces of God

Through studying and praying with some of the less known images of God that are found in the Bible, we will discover new facets of God's character that will show us more of the length and depth and breadth and height of God's love for us.

5. Exploring the Feminine Face of God

There is a subtle but strong strand throughout the Bible of feminine images of God. We will explore these and pray using them.

C. SEXUAL ABUSE

1. Is Nothing Sacred?

Sexual Abuse in the church community. For clergy, partners, elders. We will look at the incidence, the causes, and the effects of clergy sexual abuse. Then work with how we can be responsible in this area both as individuals and a Presbyteries/UDCs. This could be a presentation to a Presbytery/UDC.

2. For Survivors of Sexual Abuse by Church Leaders (Survivors only)

A 'private meeting' with women only, who have been abused by clergy/leaders. Back up will need to be provided.

3. God Who Are You?

A seminar on the effects of sexual abuse on women's experience of God. Suitable for spiritual directors, therapists, counselors, and clergy.

• • •

As Warren had died six years before, when I visited the Presbyteries around the country I took as my support, the two Catholic Sisters I worked with at The Still Point – Yvonne Munroe and Judith Anne O'Sullivan. These two amazing women took it in turns to travel with me and helped run the workshops. I felt it was a great witness to the fact that we were 'One Body.' I loved going into the parishes and saying, "I have bought as my support Judith Anne, or Yvonne, who happens to be a Catholic Sister."

The workshops that I remember most, were the ones where we were able to move more deeply into our experience of God, through learning new ways of praying and recognising our own life stories as scripture for us. The times when I met gay people and their relatives, and others who have been abused by some of us in leadership roles, certainly gave me a fuller, if more painful picture of this church.

Face to Face

A Kit of Resources prepared to encourage dialogue about the issue of homosexuals in leadership of the Presbyterian Church of Aotearoa New Zealand.

The Kit has been prepared by the Right Rev. Margaret Schrader.

As part of my offering to the church, I initiated a major consultation process with parishes across the country to discuss and address the dissention regarding homo-sexuality in leadership. Working in partnership with representatives from the parishes we began the debate, developed a process flow chart, and prepared a Kit of Resources called *Face to Face*, which was used to encourage dialogue between people of different perspectives within the Presbyterian Church.

The Face to Face Kit of Resources

There were common misconceptions about homosexual people that needed to be explored. One of the misconceptions was that, 'Christians are united in their opposition to homosexual people and homosexuality.' A letter to the editor for *Crosslink* reported on the experience of participating in these workshops.

> "Regarding Margaret Schrader's 'Face to Face,' thank you to Margaret for the way in which she presented this study. 25 members of our parish participated in the six two-hour studies. The series is thought provoking and soul searching, and we all completed the study realising how difficult it is to make a 'yes' or a 'no' assessment which answers the questions. May we commend this study to every parish in New Zealand, that every person eligible to vote at Assembly on the issue of ordaining homosexual people, can do so having at least examined the differing points of view."

A group of key people – including me (as the Moderator), the Moderator Designate and the Assembly Executive Secretary – continued to meet to seek agreement on a process for the 1996 Assembly. Other members of the wider group shared in the discussions by letter and telephone calls.

Inevitably, there was heated debate as the different perspectives were aired. As a result, it was felt that total agreement on a whole process would be impossible. Subsequently, I invited a group that included the leaders of each side of the debate to come on a retreat at the Home of Compassion. I used a family therapy model when we talked honestly about:

- How we personally felt about the issue.
- Our own backgrounds and what the biblical themes were that influenced our personal stance.
- How we felt when this was discussed.
- A way forward

We read biblical material, shared our personal perspectives, and shed many tears through the process. Although we had come a long way and were feeling good about the work we had done, the Church wasn't quite ready. We left having decided as a group that we would take a motion to Assembly stating that each church could make a decision for themselves, i.e.

- Yes, we are happy to have a gay minister, or

- No, we do not want a gay minister.

I left the retreat feeling that this was a good way forward for all of us.

Unfortunately, a few days after I arrived home, I had a phone call from one of the members of the group. He said, "Marg I am so sorry. When I told our group what we had decided, they told me that I had been brainwashed. So, it's no use bringing this motion to Assembly." It was disheartening to receive this feedback.

Eventually, the Business Committee recommended a process to take the debate to the next level.

The first question for the Assembly was:

"Does the assembly agree to place the matter of homosexuality on its agenda for discussion?"

If the answer was 'No,' did the Assembly want a referendum?

If the answer was 'Yes' – four indicative positions were offered for consideration. In brief these were referred to as follows:

Position A

The Assembly determines that the PCANZ will not permit its courts to license, ordain, or induct practicing homosexuals to the ministry of Word and Sacraments and the office of elder.

Position B

That the Assembly determines that the courts of the PCANZ will license, ordain and induct students, licentiates, ministers of Word and Sacraments, elder-elect and elders without discrimination on the ground of homosexual orientation or practice.

Position C

That the Assembly determines that:

a. A Presbytery may refuse to license, ordain, or induct a practicing homosexual person on the grounds that he/she is a practicing homosexual

b. A Presbytery may refuse to ordain, or admit to the eldership, a practicing homosexual person.

c. A presbytery may license, ordain, or induct a practicing homosexual person.

d. An appeal or complaint by may be made against the decision of a Presbytery or Session to either license, ordain, or induct, or refuse to do so, on the sole ground that the student, licentiate, minister, elder-elect, or elder is a practicing homosexual.

Position D

That the Assembly acknowledge the diversity of viewpoints within the church on issues related to homosexuality, and in the light of that diversity, this Assembly resolve to take no new steps to enact regulations regarding homosexual people in positions of leadership.

In effect this fourth position would encourage continuing dialogue and growth within the church on this issue.

These were challenging times for those involved. Following the engagement process, most, but not all, of the parishes took a liberal view. The 1996 General Assembly debated the following motion:

"That Assembly, recognising the need for a clear ruling on practicing homosexuals in leadership in the Church, rules that its courts shall not licence, ordain or induct practicing homosexuals. At the same time Assembly acknowledges the deep diversity of convictions in the Church on issues relating to homosexuality generally and calls the Church to move ahead in a spirit of gracious respect and compassion for one another."

Following the debate, the ruling was that:

"The courts (the courts of the Presbyterian Church of Aotearoa New Zealand) shall not licence, ordain or induct practicing homosexuals and this matter is now referred to Presbyteries/Union District Councils, Sessions/Parish Councils under the Barrier Act."

The regulations indicated that the ruling was:

> "intended to apply to the licensing, ordination and induction of ministers and the ordination and induction of elders."

The result was disappointing, but we were not surprised with the outcome.

One of the funny things I remember most about chairing the Assembly was that someone came up to me during the homosexuality debate and said, "Marg, Kim Hill wishes to speak to you." I answered, "Please tell her I cannot speak to her now but will ring her when I'm free." When I rang Kim, she finished the interview on Radio New Zealand's Morning Report by saying, "That was Marg Schrader, the very moderate Moderator of the Presbyterian Church of New Zealand."

I had frequently wondered if I could speak my mind on where I stood. But I knew my task was to facilitate the discussion, not to take sides.

More than two decades have passed since the Assembly where the ruling was announced. In 2022, Rev Phil King advised that the latest ruling/question about gay people in ministry, according to Chapter 9 1A is:

> "(1A) Sexual relations outside marriage. In accordance with the supreme and subordinate standards of the Church, church councils and presbyteries shall not accept for training, license, ordain or induct anyone involved in a sexual relationship outside of a faithful marriage between a man and a woman. In relation to homosexuality, and the interests of natural justice, this ruling shall not prejudice anyone who, as at 29 September 2006, had been accepted for training, or was licensed, ordained or inducted."

The good news is:

> "The conversation is ongoing, and our Moderator Hamish Galloway is encouraging a conversation on inclusivity during his term over the next year."

It was a deep honour to be chosen as the third woman Moderator in the Presbyterian Church, and to this day there have only been four women Moderators. Reflecting on my Moderator memories, I consider the trips around the country, as well as to the Cook Islands and Australia, were an enormous privilege. I met with men, women and children, and young people of all shapes and sizes, races, and theological bents. Being welcomed into their hearts and their homes, hearing their joy, and their pain, is something I will never forget.

Thank you, Presbyterian Church of Australia, and New Zealand (PCANZ), for the privilege.

10 – The Caring Church

This talk was given in Dunedin.

May the words of my mouth and the meditations of our hearts be acceptable in your sight. Oh Lord, Our strength, and Our Redeemer.

'The Caring Church' is one of my favourite concepts and speaks of who I am and what God means to me. I was on retreat when I began to prepare for this talk. After I had done some of those other things you do on retreat, I began to pray into this talk. I had two dreams one night after another.

In my first dream, I was preaching in a small, packed church. There was a Dutch family standing up the back and I was preaching from Ezekiel about wheels. All of a sudden, a man cried out, "You are not preaching from the lectionary." I said, "Yes, I am. I am preaching from Ezekiel." Suddenly, pandemonium broke out in the church. A group of women and children came and gathered around the table from which I was preaching and accidentally I closed my Bible. Then when I tried to find Ezekiel again, I could not find it. Not even in the index.

When I woke up, my heart was pounding, my head was thumping, and I grabbed my Bible. Fortunately, Ezekiel was there. I am no biblical scholar, so, I started somewhere in the middle, thinking it is probably in the middle work towards the end, and then finally found it in chapter one. That day I devoured Ezekiel, as he was told by God to eat the paper. I did not eat the paper, but I certainly devoured Ezekiel. As I read it, I heard about the sins of the nation and in the hope that God had something to offer, I began to ask myself, "What is it? In what way am I not preaching from the lectionary? In what, why am I not really preaching what God is saying?"

As I read Ezekiel and those horrible chapters at the beginning, I began to realise that I very seldom tell how bad it is.

As I sat in my office, in my spiritual direction room day after day, I heard horror stories about the church. I felt as though I was on the edge of the church. I certainly listened to many people who were struggling as to whether they can remain within the church. When I was Moderator, I was right in the centre of the church – it was a long trip and I saw an enormous amount about how the church cares. And we have all got our own stories about what a caring group of people we are within the church. We hear of people who organise housing for the poor of people, who care for children. You know the stories – I do not need to tell you. But what I am sensing I need to say, is to tell you some of the stories that I heard on the edge of the church. Particularly the stories of values of those who feel that they can no longer stay within the church that they have loved all their life – the church that has nurtured them, the church that has been home for them.

I am not just talking about Presbyterians. Those who feel that their gifts are not wanted, that their particular call, which may be to work outside the church, is not needed. Those whose journey into God has taken them into such a deep place, that the worship that is offered in their local parish, is no longer meeting their needs.

I heard stories of people who felt that they weren't confident to talk about the way their church was going with their minister or with their elders. If they wanted to offer an opinion, they felt they may be spurned and pushed away. And sometimes, forgive us, they are told that they are not listening to God, or even that that is the work of the devil.

I heard stories of people who so love God, are so wanting to be in touch with God, and are honest and open on their journey, that they take that very, very, difficult stance and leave the church that has nurtured them and loved them.

I also heard from a lot of clergy because I supervised a lot of clergy. I heard from clergy tired or worn out, exhausted in some way or another. I have not got the exact figures, but it was suggested that somewhere like 75% of clergy are close to burnout, and if you include their spouses, the number is even higher. I heard clergy who were saying, "If I really preached what I believe I might be thrown out, or people will leave the church or not give money." I heard clergy who are so full of their own pain, that they had little energy and time for the pain of other people. It makes me mad – but I understand it. I heard clergy time and time again saying, "I cannot have a day off. I'm too busy," and we forget that this is God's church that God calls us to have Sabbath.

I see a church in which there is a lot of pain. I also see a national church that is divided and polarised. Where we call each other names. Where we somehow try to manipulate the system so that what we think is right. It happens when we have forgotten about listening to each other and are only wanting to put our own point of view across. And I cry for that church, my church, your church.

As I was working on my dream in spiritual direction, I found myself talking about the dry bones in Ezekiel. I put my hands up, to demonstrate this talk about the bones. And as I did, I was very aware that they (my hands) felt dry and misshapen, and that the marrow was dry and unable to give life. But as I held my hands like that, I had a sense that within my hands was a beating heart strong, powerful, and vibrant, that the heart of God is strong and alive.

That the structures in which we live, and work are no longer working. I think my hands were talking not only about our national strikes, and our Presbytery structures, but all of this. The structures within me and within you, that stop us from being fully the person we are in Christ. I am glad about the work we are doing as a church around national structures and Presbytery structures, and only half glad about the commission on diversity, because I am there.

We do need to change our structure. But even more, we need to be in touch with this beating heart of God, that yearns and longs for the church.

I had a second dream the next night. In this dream, I was preaching, again in a crowded church, and it was Central Baptist.

Those of you who work with dreams, know that the setting for the dream often talks about the environment in which you think you are living.

For some reason or other, I had decided that I was going to preach for 30-40 minutes. I said to the woman next to me, "How long are you expecting me to preach for?" And she said, "Oh, two to three minutes." I went into panic mode. I could not remember a thing I was going to say.

Then they welcomed the guests, and one of the guests who they welcomed was Lloyd Geering. So here was I in Central Baptist Church with Lloyd Geering sitting there.

It was about three or four o'clock in the morning when I woke with that dream. For the next few hours, I was in and out of sleep, trying to work out what I would say in three minutes to this very diverse group of people. By the time I woke up, I had decided that I was going to tell the story of the prodigal son, in modern language. As I worked on that, I began to realise how very, very, different is the God of Ezekiel and the God that Luke speaks about.

Ah, thank God!

The God of Ezekiel is the Holy God who is going to change the people and bring new hope for God's own sake. God is not going to be bargained with. God is not going to be manipulated. God will do it for God's own sake. It is an austere God – a God out there somewhere.

The God of the prodigal son is the one who stands waiting, looking, longing for his son to come. The God who picks up his skirts, runs, and says, "Come on, I am so delighted you are home. Come on, let us party." That God is full of grace, and full of yearning, yearning love for each one of us.

At the same time as I was working on these dreams, I was reading the book by Philip Yancey, *What's So Amazing About Grace.* In the first chapter of this book, Philip Yancey talks about the church. This is just one little example:

"A prostitute came to me in a wretched state – homeless, sick, unable to buy food for her two-year-old daughter. Through sobs and tears, she told me she had been renting out her daughter, two years old, to men interested in kinky sex. She made more renting out her daughter for an hour, than she could earn on her own, in one night. She had to do it, she said, to support her drug habit. I could hardly bear hearing her sordid story. For one thing, it made me legally liable. I am required to report cases of child abuse. I had no idea what to say to this woman. At last asked if she had ever thought of going to a church for help. I will never forget the look of pure naive shock that crossed her face, "Church," she cries. "Why would I ever go there?" I was already feeling terrible about myself. This just made me feel worse. Where is the God that welcomes the sinner, that loves the prostitute? And cares for the drug addict and the drug pusher? Where is the God, who in Jesus came and had parties with those who the religious ones pushed to the edge? Where is God whose grace continues to say, 'Come I am here. I want to have a meal with you. I want to enjoy you.'"

In 1994, I was nominated as Moderator in Wellington. Martin Stewart reminded me of the night I made my acceptance speech. I suggested to the church that our God is a God who always finds a way through that. There is always a third way, and I gave three examples:

- When the Israelites were at the Red Sea, and God opened it.
- When Joseph did not know what to do about Mary, and God showed him a new way.
- When the church was struggling with the issue of circumcision, and God showed a new way.

The following day, Martin came to me (I have his permission), and said, "Marg, I had a dream." (I am not the only one that gets dreams). "And I think it is about the new way, the third way, but I am not ready to tell you about it at the moment." I said, "Thank you. Please feel free to come and tell me anytime you like, or to write to me."

Four and a half years later, Martin came to me and said, "I am now ready to tell you about the dream."

Martin was in the assembly. The assembly was talking about 'the issue,' which we are not allowed to talk about because there was a Rāhui. There was a lot of anger. There was a lot of pain, and there was a lot of the church being as bad as the church can possibly be. And Martin was dressed in his clown costume. He told me, he is an "Easter Saturday clown" – the clown that waits in the pain, not knowing what the future's about. He moved into the queue waiting to come to the microphone, and when he got to the microphone, he opened his mouth to speak, and began to cry. He stood there, and he cried, and cried, and cried. The green light turned to yellow, and the yellow light turn to red, and he sat down. There was some laughter and there were some angry sounds from people saying, "Why are you wasting our time?"

A few people later, somebody else stood up to speak. He stood there in silence for his whole three minutes, and then he sat down. As people continued to speak, one after another, all around the assembly, people stood in silence, until the debate was over, knowing that they had nothing to say and that they needed to go home. They were not able to speak about the issue.

As a church, we have been gifted by the tangata whenua with this gift of Rāhui. A gift of time to be silent. A gift of time to be quiet – to be cleansed and to be replenished. For those of you who do not know what Rāhui is, it's a Māori word. When our waterways have been polluted, or our land has been polluted, they call a Rāhui for the land to replenish itself, or for the waterways to replenish itself. The tangata whenua gifted it to us at that assembly. We have a Rāhui, where we are being called to be quiet and to pray. It is a Rāhui, which will give us time to do that deep inner journeying into ourselves, and into our God. A time when we forget our arguments and forget wanting to talk organised structures that will suit us, and a time when we can go deep within ourselves.

We can discover again the God of Ezekiel that says, "I will do what I will do." And the God of Luke who says, "Come I am here. I am waiting for you. I love you." It's a time when we can go within ourselves and find our own pain and deal with it. When we can name our own woundedness, and open that to healing. God opened that woundedness, which so often stops us from being church. Or that fear or that pain that stops us going to somebody whom we have hurt, or someone who has hurt us. For some of that pain, some of that woundedness, we will need to sit with a skilled therapist, or a spiritual director, to have it healed. This is a time to go inside ourselves – into that stillness, and discover again that we are one, that my pain and your pain are very, very, similar. And that gives us the courage to meet each other.

We have been gifted with Rāhui. We have also been gifted with a time to be together. And the commission on diversity are going to do a whistle stop tour all around the church – listening. When we have done that deep inner journeying – to find again the strength that is ours in God, to define that gift, that giftedness that is ours, and to claim it – we will find again the call that is on our life, and will move out into that call. We will find again the courage to say, "No," to all those things that fill our lives and stop us from doing the thing, which is our thing, that particular part of life that God has called us to do.

We need to journey from that deep inner place to a place of community, a place where we can do our forgiving, do our encouraging, where we begin to gossip about our call and say to each other, "Hey, I am really interested in working on land issues," or, "Hey, I am really interested in working with halfway people from the psychiatric units," or whatever it is. We can discover again, those other people who are there, who have a similar call, so that we can share together that call, and move out from there in the sense of community where we find encouragement from each other. Where we can be held accountable. Where we can be listened to and loved into a new place. We cannot be Christians on our own – for goodness' sake. It is an old saying, but it is even more true than it ever was today.

From there, we need to move out into the world, doing those things, which God has called us to do, offering those gifts, which God has gifted us with – and they will be very different. If we are to be a caring church – and that was the topic – each of us needs to be doing our part. And for each of us, it will be different. One of my calls was to The Still Point. I was there because I loved doing that work, was energised by it.

Although I am interested in land issues, you are never going to see me making a speech about it. I find it very, very difficult to be with people who are very, very, sick, severely disabled, or mentally ill. I have not got that patience. And yet there are many of us for whom that is an absolute delight, an absolute joy, and they will be energised in doing it. The call on our lives comes out of our own deep longings and our own pain. Somehow, as we discover that call and begin to answer, we are energised in the doing. It is our own good work.

I want to go back to Ezekiel. After Ezekiel had spoken about how bad the world was, there was a time when God stopped him from speaking. He was made numb – a little bit like the Rāhui. He was there in that voiceless place, when a messenger came and said, "The city has fallen. Jerusalem has fallen." Then Ezekiel began to speak again. He was able to talk first about how bad it was, and unfortunately, that very harsh chapter about the shepherds; then he was able to give the message of hope. The message of God bringing cleansing to our hearts; washing our hearts so that we take away the heart of stone and find a heart of flesh.

God will do it in God's good time. The message about the dry bones, these bones that are not able to encapsulate the heart, which stop the heart from doing what it needs to. That God will blow new life into those dry bones and make the flesh dance, bringing energy, excitement, and a sense of being God's people. After that, there are just a few verses, where God tells Ezekiel to pick up two sticks, and suggests to Ezekiel to, "Take one stick and call it Israel, take the other stick, call it Judah, and put them together, and I will make one people."

Does this have something to say to us at this moment? This is not going to happen unless we allow our souls to be broken. Unless we do that deep, inner journey into what it is that keeps us apart. Wherever we stand, and many of us are in the middle, we are still separate. God made a promise to Israel and Judah, and that promise still holds – that we will be one people.

Then on to that wonderful picture of the temple, out of which streams of living water will flow. With every ounce of my being, I feel that where we are as a church at this moment, is the place where God has called us. When we name our pain, and our confusion, and our anger, and our rage, and our fury, and our despair, and our sadness, and our hopelessness – they are all the words I have heard as we have looked at our church – when we name that, that is when God is able to act. Because that is where we are, in the reality of our lives

God somehow meets us in the confusion. God meets us in the pain. God meets us in the desperation. Not when we are working about issues and structures. I know God, of course, meets us there too. In reality, the change, and the hope can only come when we name it as it really is and allow the God to come and to be God, so that we can hear the bones begin to rattle and see the flesh begin to form. Where we can experience that our hearts of stone have been made into hearts of flesh. And then we will recognise the water that is flowing again from the temple to bring healing to the nations.

11 – The Effect of Sexual Abuse on Women's Naming and Experiencing of God

Counselling has been an integral part of my life. After my time as Moderator, I continued my work as a spiritual director/retreat giver and offered counselling, using the family therapy model I previously mentioned. My favourite image for this work is that it is like being a 'midwife to the soul.' I loved the one-to-one work as people explored the movement of the Spirit in their lives and grew in God, discovering more and more of the mystery that is God and the deep love God has for them.

I worked with the Accident Compensation Corporation (ACC) for a while with victims of abuse. Over time, I began working with women who had been sexually abused by their fathers or by their 'fathers in God', (i.e. their church ministers). I discovered how important it was for some of them to be given biblical words and images for God that were non-male. So, I introduced them to some of the rich biblical words and images of God, such as God as the 'midwife' who helps us through the deep painful labour of new birth.

Much is spoken of the effects of sexual abuse these days, particularly its effect on the body and mind of the victim. A few years ago, I wrote a paper for spiritual directors, addressing the way it affects women's spiritual lives, their naming of God, and the ways they relate to God, and others, and to themselves. This was my final paper for Shalem, where I had completed my Spiritual Directors training. In this context, I will share some of stories that women have shared with me, explore some theological and spiritual writings, and look at ways spiritual directors can help a person come to a new place in God.

The women I speak of in the following pages, entrusted me with their story. For obvious reasons, I have used biblical names, rather than their real names, to remind us of the many stories of abuse and rape in the Bible. Most of the women mentioned were in therapy dealing with their abuse. Each of them could see their relationship to God as an integral part of their journey to wholeness. Most of them struggled with questions like:

"Where were you, God, when this happened? Aren't you supposed to love the little children?"

"Do you have power, God? Why couldn't you have stopped this from happening?"

And the even more basic one,

"Who are you, God? What are you really like?"

As the slow and very painful journey towards healing begins to happen, these issues needed to be faced. Sexual abuse wounds not only the body and the mind but the very core of the person, the part of us that defines who each one is, the part that we call spirit, the part that longs for union with the One who is love and mercy. Many who have been abused find that they are afraid and unable to open themselves to God as a partner in the healing because they are so damaged.

Priscilla: "God is cold, hard, steel, grey," she said as she began to unfold her story of abuse in the midst of her Christian family.

Lydia: "I was overpowered, controlled, destroyed at my core by a male – a minister – who told me that, 'This is what God wants for us.' From that day I couldn't bear the thought of a male God who might want to control my life. I dropped any idea of God at all, as the only model I had was masculine. Along with the pain of the abuse, I felt this huge spiritual void within me."

Hagar: "I only discovered God years after the abuse by the males in my family had stopped. He came as benevolent Father. I could crawl up on his knee and have the fathering I so longed for. Then as I matured, I began to see him as cold, calculating, and heartless. I knew he could heal me if he wanted to, but he chose not to. Today, he is Lord, there is no fight in me now with him, he embraces me with love and care. Even though it was males that sexually abused me, it was my mother who constantly raped my psyche, refusing to believe my reality. That's why none of the feminine images of God make any sense to me, either."

Every voice is different, every story has its own pathos, and all of them have their own ways of describing this God who comes in mystery to each of us.

Tamar: Tamar was abused by her brother. Her mother knew but denied knowing because, "It would upset Father," and it was important to keep his world secure. Tamar knew that Father was the one around whom the painful world of her childhood revolved. Trying to keep her distance from her father, she did the same with God. "For me, God does not exist."

Phoebe: A very committed full-time Christian worker, theologically trained, Phoebe verbalised a belief in a God who loved her and was active in the healing process. But when she was in the midst of working on the abuse, that is not how she experienced God. The God of her early childhood looked down on her with a black book in hand and punished her if she was naughty. To have been abused meant that she was very bad and therefore must be very silent about this pain and, with everything that is within her, and keep this area hidden from God.

So speak some of the women who came to work through the horrors wrought by sexual abuse. Every voice is different, every story has its own pathos, and all of them have their own ways of describing this God who comes in mystery to each of us.

Our Images of God Shape Our Identity

Elizabeth Johnson, in her book, *She Who Is*, writes:

> "The symbol of God functions as the primary symbol of the whole religious system, the ultimate point of reference for understanding experience, life and the world. Hence, the way a faith community shapes language about God ... moulds the corporate identity and directs its praxis. Neither abstract in content nor neutral in its effect, speaking about God sums up, unifies and expresses a faith community's sense of ultimate mystery, the world view and expectation of order devolving from this, and the concomitant orientation of human life and devotion." (p. 3-4).

If we believe in a warrior God, we will become a warlike people. If we believe in a God who is all compassion, we will in turn desire to grow in compassion. If we believe in a God who has punished, wounded or been unfeeling, we will grow to be the same. The abuse that many of these women have experienced, shattered their concept of God as loving and caring. They internalised and introjected their concept of this harsh God by being very harsh on themselves.

Phoebe said, "Perhaps if I give myself a hard enough time, then God won't need to punish me so much." Priscilla had a God who is cold and hard and unfeeling. She cut herself off from all feeling even to the point where she blanched if I asked what was happening in her body or mentioned that she was a woman. Ruth mutilated her own body. This physical pain released her, if only momentarily, from the psychic, spiritual pain that was every present.

A survivor's internal dynamic with God will also affect the way she relates to those around her.

How Do We Name God?

Martin Luther said,

"God is that to which your heart clings and entrusts itself."

No wonder women ask the question, "How do we name God?" The symbol of God that the name evokes has a powerful function. If I believe that God is almighty and all-powerful and has, therefore, chosen sexual abuse for me, then I relate to God in fear and sometimes horror, walking away as Tamar has done. I may remain very afraid, becoming subservient to those around me, which is what Priscilla did. I may try desperately never to make a mistake as Chloe has done, because she knows she will be punished if she does. Because God is so central in our lives, our view of God affects everything we do and say and think.

What then is the effect on sexually abused women whose healing is tied up in their acceptance of their womanhood and their sexuality and their power to take control of their own lives? What if they have been brought up with the primary image of God as male who, however loving, is often strong, judging, and demanding of our obedience?

Dorothee Soelle puts it this way in, *The Strength of the Weak: Toward a Christian Feminist Identity,*

"As a woman I have to ask why it is that human beings honour a God whose most important attribute is power, whose prime need is to subjugate, whose greatest fear is equality… Why should we love and honor God who does not transcend but only reaffirms the moral level of our male dominated culture?" (p. 97)

Carol Christ, in *Woman Spirit Rising*, makes the point that:

"A woman may see herself like God (created in the image of God) only by denying her own sexual identity and affirming God's transcendence of sexual identity. But she can never have the experience that is freely available to every man and boy in her culture, of having her sexual identity affirmed as being in the image and likeness of God." (p. 275).

How we sense, understand, and experience God is intimately linked with all that happens in our lives and the world in which we live. Sometimes, the ways in which we name God in our prayers and our talk are more the habit of the past or the titles the church has given to God; they do not necessarily or accurately describe the God out of whom we live. The spiritual direction process can help women move beyond these old or institutional images to ones that form their lives. It is essential to invite and challenge them to name God in a way that is meaningful and real to them.

Martha struggled with this. Her abuse started when she was three months old. As an adult, after a lot of spiritual direction, her sense of God was of one who protected, nurtured, and surrounded her. The physical sense was of being 'in God.' The only word she had to describe it was 'womb,' the one place in her life where she had known safety. But she was embarrassed to speak of it for it seems so different from the images she had heard in church and read of in the Bible. She worried that 'womb' was, in some way, a bad image. She was thrilled when she was introduced to Phyllis Tribble's work on the Hebrew word for womb, *rehem*, the singular for *rahamim*, which means compassion, mercy, and love – that wonderful word that is repeated so often to describe God (*God and the Rhetoric of Spirituality*, p. 38).

Later, she discovered Paul's description of God, "in whom we live and move and have our being." For Martha, it was important that her image was Biblical. Others are discovering that God uses many sources to speak. Creation, other people, dream images are but a few.

For abused women in particular, care needs to be taken to help them name God, as God seems to be for them in this present moment.

For many, the dichotomy between a loving all-powerful God who protects them and their experience of abuse is marked. The traditional mainly masculine Father, Lord, and King are very scary because the primary males in their lives abused them and 'lorded' it over them. These women search for feminine ways to name God, but they often find that this takes an act of courage, especially if they come from a church that denies the numerous biblical references to Wisdom, the Shekinah, the woman who gave birth to humanity, (Deuteronomy 32:18); the midwife God, (Psalm 22: 9-10); the mother, (Isaiah 66:11-12) and (Isaiah 49:15); the mother eagle, (Deuteronomy 32: 11-12); the woman who searches for her lost coin, (Luke 15:8); and so on.

For others where the abuser was a woman, the move toward speaking of God in more feminine terms seems abhorrent. For abused women in particular, care needs to be taken to help them name God as God seems to be for them in this present moment.

The Way to Healing: Knowledge of Self, Knowledge of God

Many women who have been sexually abused need to express the truth of their reality. They are angry with and disappointed in God. For some this is frightening and goes against all their conditioning. Many choose to walk away or hide their true feelings. Others find it too difficult to face, and spiritual directors need to give people all the time they need to entrust their life to God.

But in the end, it is Jesus who speaks a trustworthy psycho-spiritual reality, "The truth will set you free." (John 8:32).

It is the testimony of many of the saints and mystics of the past that, the way to God is intimately linked with the path of self-knowledge. Catherine of Sienna talks about the cell of self-knowledge:

> "Let us enter the depths of that well, for if we dwell there, we will necessarily come to know both ourselves and God's goodness."

Notably, as Julian of Norwich tells her story about God and herself in, *Revelations of Divine Love*, as the number of images of God as female increases, there is a marked decrease in disparaging comments about herself. As her image of God expanded, Julian's self concept became stronger and more secure.

As women who have been abused face honestly and truthfully into their darkness of their experience and the darkness of God, they grow and their relationship to God also grows. It seems that a wonderful interplay happens between the images we have of ourselves and the images we have of God. As women begin to love themselves more and claim more of their own power, they become more open to the idea that God, too, is loving. At other times, God can be named as woman, midwife, etc. This naming begins the process of growth toward an acceptance of themselves as woman and as sexual – they begin to know the real truth about themselves.

As Mary said, "...since I have been working on this stuff I have discovered more of God, but I have become less Christian!" When we explored what she meant, she spoke of how knowing more of God's love for her, helped her to learn to love herself more, and not constantly focus on herself as a sinner. She also gave away some of the judgmental attitudes she had towards people who were not acceptable in her particular church. Her attitudes concerning some of the big issues of the day changed and she found herself to be more inclusive and loving.

Changing Images of God

The work of searching for new images of God is important yet threatening for those who are brave enough to begin the journey. They know their images of God no longer work for them, but they are concerned about whether new images might move them into heresy, or where this might take them in relation to their church, particularly those from more conservative churches. Most also recognise through the healing process, that they need to name God anew with images or metaphors that speak of their truth.

Constance Fitzgerald, in her brilliant article, *Impasse and Dark Night*, writes of the way in which many women seem to have moved into a place of the Dark Night of the Soul. She suggests that this is a time when all our symbol systems seem to have broken, when we are faced with personal and global suffering, when we no longer feel we can trust the hierarchies that are in control, and when the traditional ordering of life seems insufficient and subordinating – God, man, woman, child, animals, plant life, etc. The God that we have been taught about no longer seems to adequately describe our experience or our deep knowledge of ourselves and God.

Fitzgerald reminds us that John of the Cross is at pains to show how our images of God are progressively and of necessity changed and shattered by life experience.

"We make our God or gods in our own image."

It is out of the pain and the darkness of our lives that our desires for God are purified and we are often stripped of those things, including our images, that stop us from relating in naked faith to the Holy One. In every relationship we come to the point where we need to withdraw our projections and recognise the mystery of the other. This is so particularly in relationship with God.

Many women who have been sexually abused, need to express the truth of their reality: They are angry with and disappointed in God.

The Use of Language and Metaphor in Naming God

No one can create images of God. Religious symbols are born and die in a culture for complex reasons. At most we can be aware of them, as they arise within the culture and within ourselves. We can grow to see images of and hear names for God which have that powerful ring of truth for us.

Sallie McFague, the American feminist, and Christian theologian, wrote of the increasing realisation of the power of language as the most distinctive attribute of human existence and how we construct our world from it. Theological constructions need to be like houses that we live in for a while, with windows partly open and doors ajar. These constructions become prisons when they no longer allow us to come and go, to add a room or take one away or, if necessary, to move out and to build a new house. McFague suggests that each generation must do theology differently. Scripture does metaphorical theology appropriate for its day.[2]

We need to take scriptural texts as a model for how to do theology appropriate for our day. As St John wrote in his context, using different images than Matthew, and Matthew used language and images different to Paul's. Theologians through the ages have continued the process as they have taken the truth of the Gospel and spoken about it in ways that would be heard in the context of their time.

Why Use Metaphors for God?

Sallie McFague, in speaking of the metaphors that we use to describe God, reminds us that a metaphor is a word, or a phrase used inappropriately. It belongs properly in one context but is used in another, e.g. the arm of the chair, war as a chess game, God as Father. What a metaphor expresses cannot be said directly or apart from it; if it could, one would have said it directly. Metaphor is a strategy of desperation. It is an attempt to say something about the unfamiliar in terms of the familiar, to speak of what we do not know in terms of what we do know. Of course, so many metaphors have become so much a part of the language that we forget they are figures of speech.[3]

Metaphors always have an 'is' and an 'is not' character. To speak of God as mother is not to define God as mother or to assert identity between God and mother; it is rather to speak of that which is almost unspeakable through the metaphor of mother. All talk of God is indirect and partial. Our images of God are formed in many ways – through what we are taught, the way our parents treat us, the stories that we are read, and our own direct experience of life and reflections on that.

If a young girl has been brought up to pray each night that her loving God will protect her from all harm and then she is abused, what does she do with that?

If God has been described as one who cares for God's own and punishes those who do not believe or who are not good, the sexually abused child has to determine not only who he or she is and what God thinks of them, but also who this God is. Do they believe what their parents and teachers have told them, or do they throw out all belief in God? Deep down, they will perhaps unconsciously begin to form within them what feels like the real picture of God, coming from what they know and have experienced.

After Priscilla had explored with me what it meant for her to have a God who felt, "cold, hard, and steel grey," I suggested that she begin to imagine that God might be pink, soft, and fluffy. She commented, "When you prayed with me last time, I thought your perception of God was different to mine. I can't believe God is like that." Of course, God is not warm, pink, soft, and fluffy; this is a very limiting view of God, but somehow, in a very wonderful way that description began to work healing within Priscilla. She returned the next week with a smile on her face and said, "I saw the warm, pink God everywhere last week – in the blossom, in the baby's face, in the flowers. Pink quietens my soul. I do not need to be afraid." At the time, Priscilla told her two young daughters about the pink God. One of her children said, "My God is yellow, like a daffodil and like the sun," – the 'is' and 'is not' of a metaphor.

Slowly the change of metaphor worked its way within Priscilla. She came in one day just before Christmas, feeling very fragile and in a dangerous place. God felt distant and judgmental. As she left, I was concerned for her safety. On her way home in the car, she put on the radio and listening to the carols, something moved within her. "God as a baby! I know about babies. I know how to relate to them. Is this God weak and vulnerable like my child? Does God then understand when I feel small and helpless?" The 'is' and 'is not' of our metaphors! Every metaphor has the ability to shock – this comes from the 'is not' of it.

All language of God is adverbial: It describes how we relate to God, and how God relates to us. It does not define God. As definitions, 'rock' and 'lover' are mutually exclusive; as models, they are mutually enriching. Each generation of people needs to speak again of God and God's way of salvation in ways that come out of their time, as Augustine and Aquinas and Luther did. Women, particularly those who have been sexually abused, have an urgent need to do this.

Jesus

For many women who have been abused by a male, the very masculinity of Jesus becomes a problem. For others, the compassionate way in which Jesus met with and freed women in the gospels is a source of healing for them in the present. Julia, severely abused within her family, found herself afraid of touch, and even flinched when someone, (whom she knew on an intellectual level would not hurt her), reached out to her. On the other hand, she had a desperate longing to be held. In the stories of the woman at the well and the bleeding woman who touched Jesus' garment, she found an acceptance and a love that she needed. As she put herself into these stories, she discovered herself. While first ashamed and frightened, she was slowly able to look Jesus in the eye and see his acceptance and then let him touch her, and from there, in very small steps, she began to allow others to touch her.

Others find the masculinity of the human Jesus too much to bear. Eve's story particularly comes to mind. She was frequently raped by her minister father in her bedroom while the traditional picture of Jesus hung on the wall. For many of these women survivors, focusing on God or the Spirit may be more helpful, as might be using some non-human images, both Biblical and other.

Wisdom

There are a growing number of women to whom Wisdom has made herself known. That wonderful feminine presence so central to the Biblical witness of God got lost in the traditional teaching of the church. Wisdom is she who was there with God from the foundation of the earth, who plays with God in creation, who stands at the city gates and yells (Proverbs 8).

Chloe, who had been focusing on Jesus in her prayer, discovered Wisdom in Proverbs 8 and it raised for her issues of her own power.

> "As I pray to God imagining him as male or to Jesus, I somehow expect to be rescued, for something to happen to me from the outside that will make it all right. I have a completely different experience when I think of Wisdom. It's as though she empowers me to be me. Together we can face the pain, discover new strategies. We women can get through this."

Lydia recalled that a week after she was abused and her images of God were shattered, she was gifted with a wonderfully strong feminine presence. This feminine presence was for her very healing.

"She touched me and moved me and affirmed me as a woman, at a time when I felt all the men I knew were controlling me, even if from the best of motives. It was as though she came and set my imagination on fire. I saw possibilities for healing that I could not have dreamed of. For the first time in my life, I had a sense of the presence of God, with hands gently laid on my shoulders calling me, 'Daughter mine.'"

Two years later she had an experience of Wisdom, a sense of the Holy One dwelling within her and offering gifts of acceptance, love, wisdom, and empowerment. This presence named herself as 'Ashdeva,' the spirit rising from the ashes. Lydia's life is testimony to the healing power of God who does make all things new.

Constance Fitzgerald has discovered that John speaks of Sophia more frequently than of God the Father. The contemplative tradition whereby we are open to the influence of God at such a deep level, seems to open the way for Sophia to come and lead us into new and radical ways of experiencing, thinking, and naming God. Women who have been thrust into the darkness of abuse, and hence thrust into questioning so much of the foundations of their life, discover, during the imprisonment of pain and the shattered dreams of life, that our gracious, gentle yet strong God comes in so many ways to say, "Hey, I'm here and I want to love you. I cry with you in your pain, and I want to be with you in your healing."

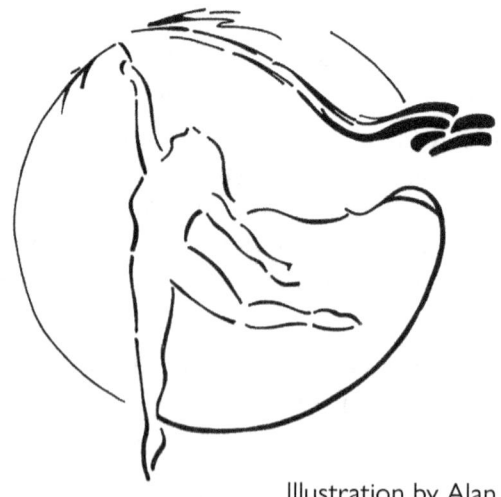

Illustration by Alan Colavecchio

Nature

Many find new meaning in images from nature that remind them of the suffering of Christ and the compassion of God. Chloe, walking along angry at God for not doing anything, was stopped in her tracks by the sight of a tree wounded by a powerful storm, with sap pouring from it. As she watched it and wondered, she heard these words within her, "He was wounded for our transgressions, he was bruised for our iniquities." (Isaiah 53:5). She had an overwhelming sense that Jesus not only knew about her suffering but had also been abused and violated. Chloe's healing had begun with a dream where God came to her as a tree, and very gently wrapped her face around with a leaf.

Rachel, walking through the bush, crying for herself and her wounded children, felt the soft rain coming down on her head and began to wonder if God perhaps cried for her? The only image of God that did not terrify Eve was that of Living Water, washing away the stain, the pain, and the utter degradation that she constantly felt. Deborah got in touch with God's compassion in an imaginative prayer exercise as she saw God as a weeping willow, and she was a small weeping cherry.

Issues of Power: God's and Ours

When a child or an adult woman is abused, she feels powerless to stop the violence to her body and mind. She is afraid that whatever she does to stop it may make things for her and her loved ones much worse. She sometimes learns that the wisest way for her at that moment is to submit and let the abuser do what he or she wants. She may be afraid that the family will break up, or that she will not be believed and therefore be ostracised, or that there may be more abuse. Threats often accompany sexual abuse. These often have the strength of a curse on the person. Therefore, she often chooses what seems the safest way to cope, which is to give up any power to speak or act in her own self defence.

In relationship to a woman's own sense of powerlessness, questions come about God's power. If God is all-powerful, then what does God think of me that God has allowed this to happen? Or, is God a whimp? Or, has God really died? What is God's place in the world? These are important theological and pastoral questions about God's identity and power. How do we speak of it? In this context, Elizabeth Johnson raises the important question, "Is the kenosis of God not only in Jesus but as an important way in which God chooses to be in the world?" Johnson reiterates Elie Weisel's terrifying question,

> When a woman is raped and murdered, what does the Shekinah say? The Shekinah says, 'My body is heavy with violation.' Through the long night when the Bethlehem concubine is gang raped and tortured, where is God? She is there being abused and defiled … Along with all abused women these women are *imago Dei*, *imago Christi*, daughters of Wisdom Sophia. God enters into the pain of women whose humanity is profaned and keeps vigil with the godforsaken for whom there is no rescue. In turn, their devastation points to the depths of the suffering. (Johnson. p. 264).

It is important to put words about the suffering God in context for women because, for many years, suffering has been something they have been asked to choose. They have been encouraged to be passive, to put aside their own giftedness and submit to men and to those in authority, denying their own truth, refusing to allow their own reality the light of day. Sometimes we speak of God's power in ways that encourage passivity. Many women are urged by pastors of conservative churches to remain in the home and love and submit to the husband who rapes them.

We need to find new ways of talking about power. Johnson says that speaking of the suffering of God has the power to unleash human compassion, responsibility, and hope.

> The dark side of such language is its potential to play into women's passive victimization by glorifying suffering. Only when set carefully and consistently in the context of a God who is utterly committed to the humanum, whose glory is the human being and specifically, women, fully alive, does the symbol of the suffering God release its empowering power. Then it signifies the power of suffering love to resist and create anew. (p. 271).

Feminist theologians are grappling for language to give voice to an understanding of power arising from women's experience, as liberation theologians are dealing with other oppressed groups. Neither "power over" nor "powerlessness," this understanding is akin to "power with."

> It is not the power of control through either domination or benevolence but the power of response and responsibility, the power of love in its various forms that operates by persuasion, care, attention, passion, and mutuality. (McFague, p. 85).

The way of being in the world is close to the way of the cross, the way of radical identification with all which the model of servant once expressed. Flora Slooson Wuellner sums up well in her theology of God's activity in suffering and healing:

> God does not send us our pain. God enters into our pain and shares it with us. God is able to bring deep healing and transformation from within. (*Heart of Healing, Heart of Light*, p. 30)

Anne Carr probes the experience of motherhood as a source of symbolising God's power, "as enablement of the autonomy of others, as gentle persuasion, as patient love and encouragement – themes consonant with the biblical descriptions of God." Relational, persuasive, erotic, connected, loving, playful, empowering, resisting – such are some of the words we seek.

Elizabeth Johnson offers more insight into the power of God:

> Holy Wisdom's 'almighty power'... is the liberating power of connectedness that is effective in compassionate love. With moral indignation, concern for broken creation, and a sympathy calling for justice, the power of God's compassionate love enters the pain of the world to transform it from within. The victory is not on the model of conquering heroism but of active, non-violent resistance as those who are afflicted are empowered to take up the cause of resistance, healing, and liberation for themselves and others. (p. 270)

Some 'How-To's' for Spiritual Directors

In being with women who have been abused, I'd like to share some of the strategies that have helped, as a trained Sexual Abuse Counsellor and Spiritual Director.

1. Be centered deeply in the love and compassion of our God so that you in turn can provide an atmosphere of safety and love.

2. Be prepared to take time. It often takes a long while to build up enough trust to tell the story. The director/directee

relationship may be the first sign for them that God is on their side.

3. Listen to and believe the story. Sometimes the story is so horrific you may find it difficult to believe. This ministry keeps us in touch with the evil of the world.

4. Constant supervision is a must; this work can eat into the soul. Make sure you have someone with whom you can share your horror and deal with your own fears, who will remind you of the presence of God.

5. Remember Jesus' words that, "the truth will set you free." (John 8:32) This is important for you and for the directee.

6. Listen carefully under the words for the image of God out of which the directee really lives. It may be very different from that which she verbalises or even thinks.

7. As you listen, be listening to the Spirit for the way through, which is unique for everyone. It may be a new biblical image of God. It may be that they have shared an experience in which they can perceive God, and which needs to be drawn out.

8. Pray with and for the directee, always checking this out with her beforehand. Use verbal or silent prayer for healing, cleansing, forgiveness, anointing with oil, and other symbolic gestures like washing. Share with them the knowledge that you hold them in prayer during the session and afterwards. Continue to remind her that God is active in the healing process.

9. Encourage honesty before God. This may mean sharing their anger and fear with God and can be very demanding.

10. Use scripture passages that tell of God's love for the hurting. Using the Ignatian method. Passages like the woman with the haemorrhage and Jesus touching the Leper can be very powerful.

11. When the directee is struggling to speak and the words won't come, offer paper and paint or crayons to, "draw what is happening for you."

12. Sometimes, imaginative exercises like Marlene Halpin's help. (See her book, *Imagine That: Using Phantasy in Spiritual Direction*, 1982.)

13. Offer books and music tapes, CDs or digital tracks that speak of God in fresh new ways and that take seriously God and people's pain.

14. Encourage the directee to listen and watch for God in their dreams, in nature, and in their everyday experiences.

15. If you are not a therapist as well as a director, be aware that when working through these issues, women will almost certainly need some therapeutic help as well.

16. Remember, above all, that this is God's work, so relax.

In Conclusion

Journeying with these women has opened new and wonderful experiences of God's grace to me. I have seen God meet and minister to some of the most misunderstood people. I have found myself breathless with amazement that, yet again, God has brought healing.

On the other hand, there have been times when I have thought, "God, I cannot cope anymore with this pain of these horror stories." As a woman these stories affected me deeply in almost every part of my being and brought to the surface areas of abuse I have personally had to work with. This is a costly ministry.

In the beginning, I had to struggle not to think that every man I saw was a potential rapist or abuser. It has taken me a while to come back to a more balanced understanding. A whole new level of compassion and understanding of God's mercy would be required if I worked with the abusers themselves. I am left with tremendous admiration for these women. I am grateful to them for all they have taught me of the rawness of humanity and the overarching, underpinning love of God.

We began this journey with Priscilla and her cold, hard, steel grey God. It is fitting to let her have the last say. In a letter to a friend recently she wrote,

> "I'm so glad I'm losing my fear of God. I'm hungry to know more of the real God who is both male and female. I don't need to kill myself anymore. God is exciting, creative, pink, soft and gentle, a little baby, nurturing, mother hen, dancing spirit and alive."

Photographs

Driftwood

The Kererū – a pigeon native to New Zealand

With my father

Walking with Mum and Dad in Melbourne

 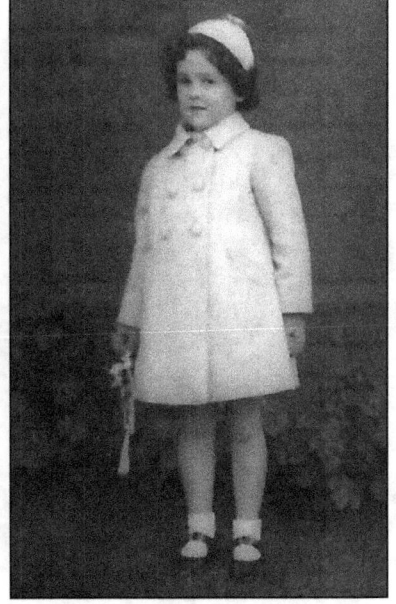

Photos of me and Mum.
Dress and coat made by mum, an amazing dressmaker

Grade 1C 1944. That's me, third from the right, second row from the top

Grade 11A 1946. I'm on the far right of the second row

My first day at intermediate school

With fellow Prefects (1955)

MARGARET STIRLING.

Margaret's claim to fame lies in the fact that she is our illustrious Head Prefect, while also being captain of the school Hockey team, Sports Editress of Record, and an ex-vice-House Captain of Hancock. "Stirl" possesses a host of peculiarities, chief amongst which is her laugh — it's a low rumble! Her good sense and reliability, coupled with her cheery disposition, have stood Margaret in good stead in her position as School Captain, and have served to make her one of the most popular girls in the school.

Vice: Secret swotting.

Favourite Sayings: "Who's on tuck?" "You're a fool!"

Theme Song: "Changing Partners".

Ambition: To get her voice to change back again.

Probable Fate: Torch singer.

"Stirl" – Head Prefect

GIRLS 1st HOCKEY.

BACK ROW: B. Lawrence, M. Cash, M. Haysom, E. Amos, P. Kilbourne, C. Steiniger, J. Corrie, R. Moy.
FRONT ROW: C. Dixon, J. Wright, B. Curnick (vice-captain), M. Stirling (captain), J. Eunson, C. Brown, V. Ring.

Hockey team: I'm the Captain in the middle of the front row

PREFECTS, 1955.
STANDING—L. to R.: A. Hannan, J. Hille, A. Rawady, J. Sheedy, J. Sprake, H. Stratos, J. Corrie, L. Cocks, A. Guthrie, M. Louey. SITTING—J. Shields, I. Wardell, M. Condie, G. Swann, J. Potter (Senior Prefect), Mr. R. E. Chapman (Principal), Miss M. Cronin, M. Stirling (Senior Prefect), J. Anderson, B. Curnick, J. Allen.

Prefects 1955. I'm fourth from the right in the front row

My big sister Joan and I at the beach

Teachers' College: That's me, fourth from the right in the front row

Our Youth Group at Croxton Methodist Church.
I'm second from the right in the middle row

Esperanza Theological College. Training with the men.
That's me, second from the right in the second row

With colleagues Ruth Arnold and Merle Harper.
Next to me is Deaconess Fisher, Warden of the Deaconess Order,
who was also in charge of Deaconess House

Studying at Esperanza with Ruth and Merle

Training to be a Deaconess.
I'm on the far right in the back row

In my uniform at Epworth Hospital

At Esperanza. Now in uniform, I'm fourth from the left in the second row

ORDAINED

Deaconess Margaret Stirling was ordained to the ministry of the Word and Pastoral Care within the Order of Deaconesses, in Wesley Church on Thursday, 14th October. This inspiring service was conducted by the Rev. R. J. Philp, President of the Conference, and the Rev. C. Gallacher, Ex-President, delivered the Charge.

1965

On Ordination day, the 14th of October 1965

Warren and the twins, Tom and Ben Schrader

60 Severn St.,
St. Albans,
Christchurch.
29.5.66

Dear Margaret,

I'm glad you are coming over to live with us. I am looking forward to coming Australia, especially the trip in the plane. The soccer ball that Dad bought me is a beauty, isn't it? On Saturday next our soccer team will be playing Shamrock, which is the top soccer team in our grade. Last Saturday we beat Celtic 9-0 and the Saturday before that we beat Wanderers 4-0. I had better go and take Kim for a walk now and try out my new soccer ball. Will write again soon.

Love
Jon.

---

60 Severn Street,
St. Albans CH.CH.
22 June 1966.

Dear Margaret,

How are you? Thank you very much for the socks. I wore them to School today and they are lovely and warm.

I have not very much to say so this well be short.

Mark likes he's fire engine very much and Jon's very pleased with soccer book.

This morning when I climbed in Dad's bed to have I cuddle I told him I could wait for the Wedding, but couldn't wait for you and Dad to get home and after school to be able to say, "Hi Mum".

I haven't any thing else to say so I will write again soon.

Love
Kay.

XXXXXXXXXXXXX

60 Severn St
Christchurch
Monday 30th

Dear Margaret,
I am very happy to have Daddy home again. I met him at the airport on Saturday night and waved to him.
I will be very happy to have you come and live with us in Christchurch. I will write you another letter later. I like my new rifle and I will not shoot you.

Love

Keir.

with Dad's help (slightly)

Dear Margaret
much ter very
for the
fire
engine
Mark
XXXXX

Four letters from the children in my family

Here we are with Warren's five eldest children

With Mum and Dad, and Warren's Mum, Molly Schrader

With our bridesmaids, my friend Jan, and Jan and Kay Schrader

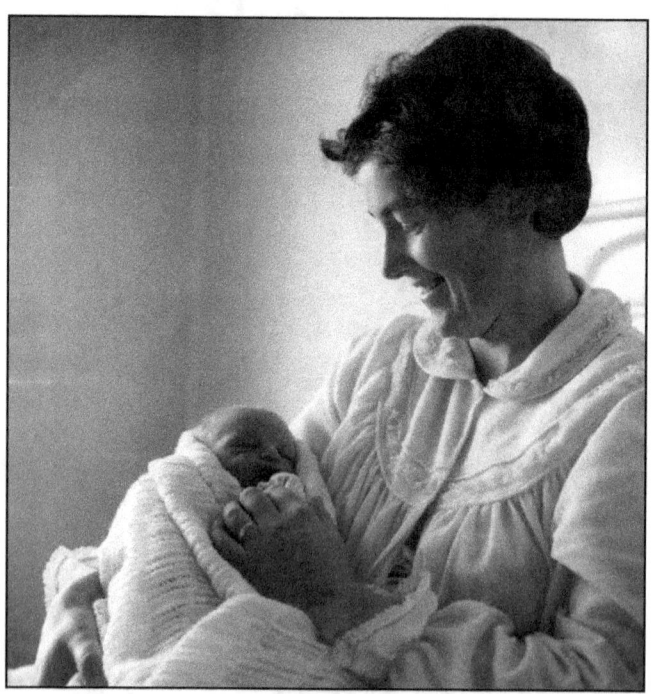

Baby Paul Schrader

Our family in Christchurch
Back row from the left Keir, Jon, and Mark
Front row from the left, Kay, Ben, Warren, To, Paul, me and Jan

Mum in later life

Elizabeth and Alan Purdie

On the right are Heather and Roger Lane
On the left are Phyllis and Bruce Purdie

Keith McEwen and Ethel Curtis

Warren and I at my ordination
at Wadestown Presbyterian Church

Rev. Lester Reid
Director of the Parish Development and Mission Department

The PDMD Team

*Photos from the Archive and Library of the
Presbyterian Church of Aotearoa NZ*

Warren graduated from The University of Otago

Mary Daish, Paul's wife in architect mode

Mary and Paul's son Zebedee at The Still Point

We danced at the opening of The Still Point

The statue outside Christ House in Washington D.C.

Judith Anne on my right and Yvonne on my left

Yvonne introduced the Clown Ministry

The wall hanging, created by Ester Willis with women from the parishes

The parishes expressed their faith

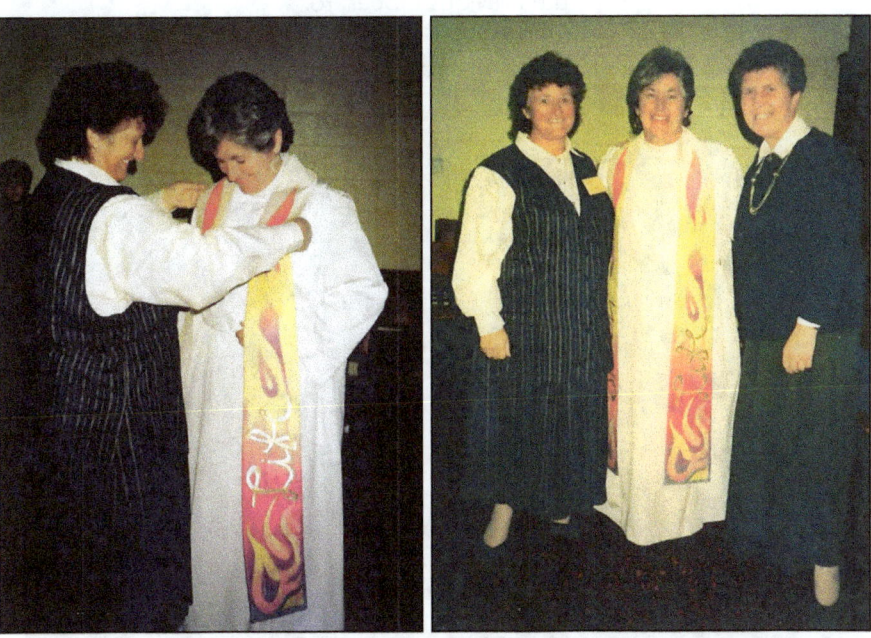

Yvonne placed the alb on me, and both she and
Judith Anne stayed with me for the service

The theme was 'One Bread One Body'
From left to right: Susan Jones and John Franklin (my two Chaplains), me,
Tame Takao Leader of the Māori Synod, and Graeme Murray,
the previous Moderator

With my family following the Induction Service

"We are a broken body. Kyrie Eleison"

Me with Tame Takao Leader of the Māori Synod,
and Michael Thawley Assembly Executive Secretary

Me with Millie Te Kaawa

The Moderators Committee 1995
Back row: Nikki Watkin, Paul Ranby, Ron McCulloch
Front row: Yvonne Munro and Judith Anne O' Sullivan

Margaret, our Moderator, calls us to support her in prayer

Please pray:

May she be filled with the knowledge of God's will in all spiritual wisdom and understanding... May she be made strong with all the strength that comes from God's power. *Colossians 1.9-11*

May God give her the tongue of a teacher, that she may know how to sustain the weary with a word and be awakened each morning to listen as those who are taught. *Isaiah 50:4-5*

May she bless God who gives her council and instructs her. *Psalm 16:7*

May she run and not be weary, walk and not faint. *Isaiah 40:31*

Moderator's Engagements 1995 - 1996

North Shore Visit
July 7 -17

Cook Islands General Assembly and Anniversary of signing of Constitution,
July 23 - August - 6

Wairarapa UDC Visit
August 11 - 21

CCANZ Forum
Christchurch, September 1 - 3

Uniting Church of Australia
Sydney, September 22 - 29

Regional Conference
Rotorua, October 27 - 29

Southland Visit
November 3 - December 4

1996

Te Hinota
Ohope, January 12 - 14

Northland Presbytery Visit
Whangarei, February 2 - 19

APW Pacific Basin Consultation
Auckland, February 29 - March 3

Christchurch Presbytery
March 8 - April 8

South Auckland Presbytery
April 21 - May 14

Programme flier

Menagerie by Joanna Braithwaite, to which I have added a Kererū.
Reprinted with the artist's permission.

The L'Arche Community on the Kapiti Coast

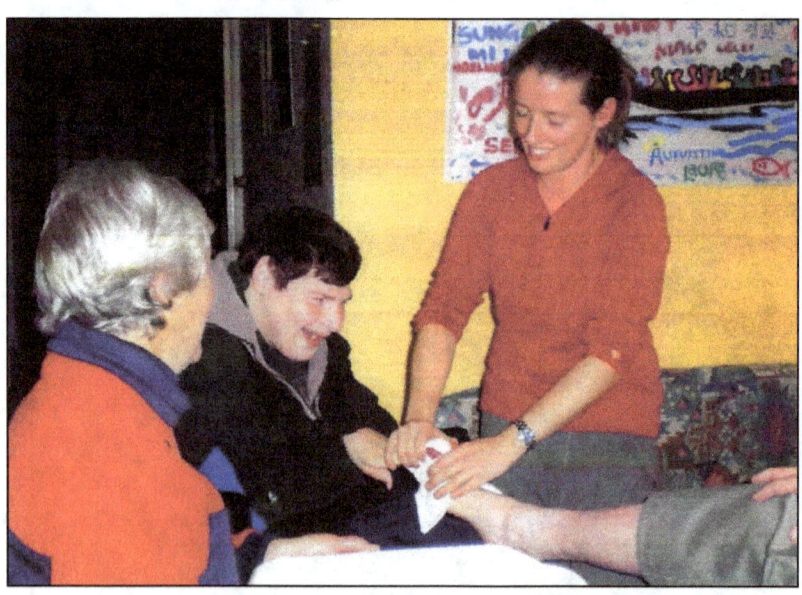

Foot Washing Victor's feet at L'Arche
With Laura one of the carers, now a Spiritual Life Coordinator

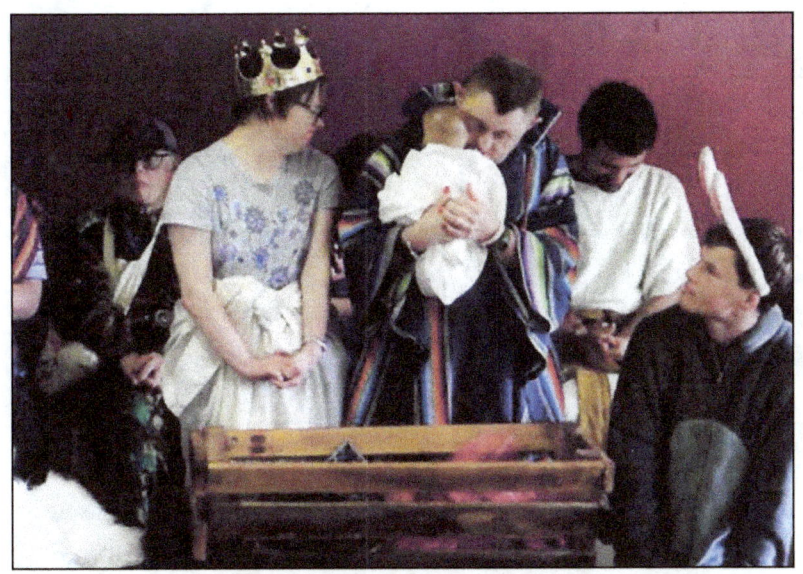

Christmas at L'Arche with Peter

Candice on the left with Laura

Kapiti L'Arche community

Mimi, my great granddaughter

L'Arche core members

Four L'Arche Assistants with Emmett

With my brother George Stirling, and sister Joan Palmer in Australia

Leaflet about The George Stirling Scholarship

One of the gardens at Parkwood Retirement Village
Photograph supplied by Marie Simpson, editor of Parkwood News.

Jon and Kimberley

12 – Dreams and Dream Therapy

My relationship with the Church may be regarded by some as unconventional. For example, I've never been invested in buildings, structures, and procedures. My ministry, with people from all walks of life, has always been, and still is, inclusive, practical, and liberal rather than traditional. Like Richard Rohr, I have always been drawn towards greater differentiation, larger viewpoints, and a deeper understanding of people. Drawing on stories from the scriptures, my own journey of development, my experience as a woman, a wife, mother, spiritual director, counsellor, and as a Moderator of the Presbyterian Church, I undertook a significant amount of work in the use of dreams in spiritual direction on spirituality.

I did most of my training in dream therapy in the United States. I've also undertaken training in New Zealand, and attended retreats focusing on dreams, including a month-long Buddhist retreat on this topic. I truly believe that God is in everything, so I went to discover more about God.

Over the years I've facilitated workshops and one-on-one sessions with individuals on dreams. As we all experience dreams, it's a topic everyone can relate to. Each night, as we sleep, we enter an altered state of consciousness, and during this period we dream. Our bodies are deeply relaxed, and we enter what is known as Rapid Eye Movement (REM) – a stage of sleep, where we experience rapid eye movement, even though our eyes are closed. During this stage, the heart rate speeds up, breathing becomes irregular and the brain is highly active. Most, but not all dreams, take place during REM sleep and during this phase the brain processes emotions.

Dreams are stories, images, thoughts, and feelings that our minds create while we sleep. The brain is not simply remembering what it has experienced during the day before. It also creates new experiences triggered by our daily lives and draws on all the sense associated with this, e.g. sounds, sights, smells, and touch. Researchers have discovered that dreaming is a vital part of how we learn. For example, we can learn a new skill one day, and get better at that skill the next day, after having dreamt about it. Somehow, the process of dreaming integrates our new experiences into our older memories. You will have heard the expression, "Sleep on it" – and often this really helps. In the morning, we may wake up refreshed, and sometimes have identified solutions to our problems.

In REM sleep, we switch off our rational conscious minds and enter a fluid space in which anything is possible. Our dreams may be insightful, creative, and fun, or they may be unsettling, disturbing, or frightening. We may not remember all our dreams, but there are occasions when we do, especially if these dreams are recurring.

Dreams often speak the language of symbolism. The events, people and things created while we sleep in our unconscious mind, are all meaningful in some way. The issue is that the meanings that arise in our dreams aren't the same meanings that arise from the way our waking mind deals with reality. Every culture through history has tried to understand the symbols used in dreams.

To illustrate, I will share examples of a few of the dreams from the scriptures. I'll also share some of the dreams I have personally experienced, in addition to the two dreams I have written about in the chapter entitled The Caring Church. Then I'll offer a model that you can use, if you are interested in working on your own dreams.

Examples from the scriptures

"We've both had dreams," they answered, "but there is no one to interpret them." Then Joseph said to them, "Do not interpretations belong to God? Tell me your dreams." (Genesis 40:8)

"When there are prophets among you, I the Lord make myself known to them in visions. I speak to them in dreams." (Numbers 12:6)

"I will pour out my spirit on all flesh. Your sons and daughters shall prophesy, your old shall dream dreams, and your young shall see visions." (Joel 2:28, Acts 2:17)

Matthew 1:18-25 speaks of the birth of Jesus and Joseph accepting that he was to be the father through a dream.

Matthew 2:12 – being warned in a dream, not to return to Herod.... they returned to their own country.

An angel of the Lord appeared to Joseph in a dream and said, "Get up, take the child and his mother and escape to Egypt. Stay there until I tell you, for Herod is going to search for the child to kill him." (Matthew 2:13)

And later in Matthew 2:19, "When Herod had died, the angel of the Lord suddenly appeared in a dream to Joseph in Egypt and told him to take the child and his mother to the land of Israel."

Matthew 27:19 speaks of Pilate's wife, "Have nothing to do with that man. I have suffered a great deal because of a dream about him."

Most of our dreams are not as clear as the dreams shown in the examples. It helps to learn how to interpret our own dreams with all the very personal symbols.

John Sanford, who wrote, *Dreams, God's Forgotten Language*, suggests that our dreams are concerned with the problem of opposites. As we explore the depths of the opposites within us, we discover we may be torn and divided between the various sides of ourselves, all of which make demands on us. It can be a frightening journey as our dreams show us the darker, weaker part of our personality, and that they too have an important role to play in the drama of our wholeness.

A competent, confident woman once shared a dream in which she was driven somewhere where she didn't want to go – in the dark. In one of her dreams, she was literally driven backwards! This is a fabulous metaphor for our shadow side – being driven where we don't want to go in the dark!

We know that God is light and goodness and love and peace, so what do we do with the darkness, the ugliness, the fear, and the violence within us? These aspects of ourselves come out in our dreams when we can no longer push them away.

We who are in Christ, have invited God into our lives, into our hearts and into our minds – and that includes the shadowy corners of our unconsciousness that emerge only when we sleep. We who are in Christ, have agreed to listen for the voice of God, whenever God communicates with us. God knows and accepts us, forgives us, and loves us, far more than we do ourselves!

The interesting question for me is what sense can we make of the symbols in our dreams? I think that you are the best person to take guesses at this for yourselves. I wonder if it's easier than we think? For example, when you describe an image in your dreams, what adjectives do you use? What in your life would you use those adjectives for? This is not about one-on-one matching, it's more about hunches. Back in the days when I often caught planes and trains, I used to dream about missing them. I would wake up very relieved that whew – I hadn't missed them at all, there was plenty of time. When I dream of rivers and water flowing, my hunch is that this represents God in some way.

Most of our dreaming is our brains tidying up, taking out the trash, reorganising our memories. But sometimes our dreams point forward, the dreams that Joseph had clearly did this. I once had a string of dreams in which I really wanted to find a boat, and when I found it, it was run down and needed work. I was sure God was telling me something, as the point of the boat was to sail away over the water.

John Sandford said,

> "God is the inner source of our life and energies, the one who speaks through our dreams, our relationships, and the events of our life. Behind all of that which we fear from our unconscious world, there is a great love; a love which pours forth out of our own soul, a love intense and demanding."

Do not fear the dark. Do not be confused by your dreams. Trust that God is at work and alive even there. God's dream speech doesn't make much sense to our rational brains. It's not as clear as Bible study, or as nice as a word of thanks from a friend. It is a language of symbols. It is entwined in a chaos of memories and emotions. It flips into fears. But it is part of who you are. Part of being human. Part of God's ongoing work in you. It's OK to dream.

An in-depth example of one of my own dreams

In a dream I had in 1987, in which I found myself in a group of people.

> We had a baby with us – small and very wise, but we were not sure where it had come from. It had a little white/grey sore patch on the back of its head. I touched it, and it said, "Ouch," and told me it was warts, and mentioned something about balloons.

It was as though we were going to start a task and this baby was our the midst, and the child was so wise. (A little child shall lead them.) The baby filled its pants, so I put it on another level, like a stage where the leaders sat, and went to get some things to clean it up. Meanwhile, the group took no notice of the child, and when I returned, it had crawled close to the edge of ledge. I grabbed it just in time.

Some thoughts

A little child will lead them. The baby is the new life, the signs of Jesus, in the Church.

Like all new babies, it needs care, love, and nurturing, and will grow at its own pace, if we look after it properly.

The dirty pants are a reminder that we all constantly need to be cleaned, even the newest signs of life.

I was holding the baby, but WE had been given it. The baby was not my baby, it is God's baby, given to us to care for. At that time, I was the one holding it. It was a gift for the whole church, and I knew I must be careful of how I fulfilled my role as the 'babysitter', and not hand it up to people whose task it is not, or who have their own babies to look after.

WE had been given the baby. There were several significant people who sense they are part of the babysitting group. I have already gathered some of these together in a group. We have called it YEAST to pray, talk and support each other.

The balloons say something about celebration of all the newness.

This dream came for me as part of an answer to the most important question for me at the time, "What is God saying to the PCANZ?" The next night, the discernment process was formulated. I believe they go together. I believe God was calling the Church to grow, to acknowledge the signs of new life and work with them.

In a dream I had in 2018, I was at a retreat or a conference, and we had been told to talk to another person.

> I know that I needed to talk about the relationship between Christianity and Buddhism and to try to understand what my role is. I look around and discover that I had nobody to talk to. Then the very young leader comes up to me and says, "Well, we can talk."

That part of the dream ends, so I get up for a while. Giving the dream some thought, I go back to bed to see if the dream continues, and it did!

> In my dream I walk northwards along a street in Auckland. I realise I have no idea where I'm going. I think I'll ask somebody, but I have no idea where I need to go, such as the name of the town. I consider ringing someone, but I have no phone on me. I know I'm fit and well and can walk easily. I'm not too worried but I do feel helpless. There is no one to help, nowhere to go, and no way to contact anybody. "God, I need you!"

Some thoughts

For some reason my sense is that the area in Auckland that I was in, was where I went to a writer's retreat.

Title (T) – Lost

Theme (T) – No obvious supports

Affect (A) – Huge questions... but not terribly worried.

Question what the dream is asking you? (Q) Where? How? Why? Who with? Is this about the memoirs? Feeling I want to give up. God help me.

In retrospect, one of the ways I have described myself is as a Dream Therapist, but I never forget that the Spirit is the real director. If you are contemplating this path, be sure to source the appropriate training. Be very prayerful. Take your time. After the training ensure that the people you work with are safe, as dreams bring up material that is previously unknown. Some dreams can take a lifetime to work on.

I offer the following model as a guide, and suggest you use this model flexibly; it is not a map! Enjoy, dreamwork is fun.

1. Tell the dream in detail.
    - Perhaps draw it. Give it a title.
    - Listen, notice your own feelings, and clarify detail.

2. Felt sense
    - Help find where in the body the felt sense is. This is that fuzzy feeling that the dream leaves.

3. Exploring

    a. Context

    - What was happening in your life at the time of the dream?

    - Any parallels?

    b. Setting or environment

    How is the setting in which the dream occurs like your life?

    c. TTAQ

    - Title

    - Theme

    - Affect

    - Question what the dream asks you.

    d. Track the dream ego

    - Identify emotions. Summarise your ego's actions. How does this compare to your normal life?

    e. Associations

    - Take each person, object, and setting; draw them and elicit the associations between dream and real life.

    - Listen for puns, metaphors, etc.

    f. Ask questions of the dream and of the characters/objects involved, e.g.

    - Why have you come now?

    - What do you want me to know?

    - How are you like me?

4. Action Work

    - Wriggle into the skin of some of the people, and the objects in the dream

    - What does it feel like?

    - What is the world like from there?

- What do you want to say to the dream ego?

- What is the dialogue between ego and dream figure?

- Always begin with a safe role in the dream.

- How is this dream connected to your life?

- Have you seen those actions, feeling, attitudes, play out in your life?

5. What is the story of the dream saying to you now?

    - If Jesus/God your dream maker were telling this story about your life, what might they be meaning?

6. Extend the dream.

    - If the dream is scary or challenging, you may wish to help them invite a wisdom figure to enter the dream with them, e.g. Jesus, Sophia etc.

Summarise and check your felt sense

- How is your body now?

- Has anything shifted?

- What are the new insights?

- Is there a call in this for you?

- What resources do you need?

- What other work do you need to do to honour this dream?

Note: Use this model flexibly. You will seldom use all of these questions and suggestions with one dream. Ask yourself, which part of the dream interests me the most? Remember this is about knowing more about ourselves and hence being able to be more fully available to God.

Let the Spirit guide.

I'll finish with a very dreamlike verse (Psalm 68:13)

> Even while you sleep among the sheep pens,
> The wings of my dove are sheathed with silver,
> It's feathers with shining gold."

May you know the touch of God's shining feathers as you sleep and as you wake.

13 – God Who Are You? Spiritual Abuse

Many of us are naming the fact that we've been spiritually abused, by parents, teachers, clergy, and house group leaders. This abuse affects the way we see ourselves, and our place in the world, our belief system, and the way we see God. I want to focus on the way abuse effects our naming and experiencing of God and, conduct an experiment in worship that helps those who have been abused.

It seems to me that the earlier the abuse happens, the greater its effects on our view of life and of God. Those of us who were abused in our early years, may not have had the discernment to recognise the power imbalance in the relationship. We find it difficult to recognise that this view is not the only one, we'll find the strength to get it out from under or challenge it.

Sometimes this abuse happens because people teach us about God who punishes, judges without compassion, who looks down from heaven with a big black book and keeps notes of all our mistakes. Other times the abuse is far subtler, not necessarily in naming God, but by the way those who do interpret God for us treat us.

Many of us describe God as loving, forgiving, just and compassionate, but when the rubber hits the road, this is not the way we perceive God. It is as though there is a second and perhaps a third level under the conscious one. That is unfortunately what motivates our lives.

I often ask people in spiritual direction what they think God is really like. "When you're vulnerable, how do you think of God?"

These are some of the answers:

> "God is like a hard steel clamp – once he gets me in his vice, he won't let me go!"

> "God is like Jekyll and Hyde, loving one moment and frighteningly manipulative the other."

> "God is against people like me. I am gay so there is no hope for me."

"My father sexually abused me, and my mother told me I was a dirty little slut and God would never forgive me. I've almost dealt with this sexual abuse, but it's the idea that God will never forgive me that frightens me the most."

"My baby died at birth and my Christian friend told me I must have done something wrong for God to punish me that way."

When we're in pain or vulnerable, other's words seem to be able to penetrate into deeper places than they would normally.

Our images of God define how we live our lives. If we live with an image of God who is loving, we are likely to be loving and secure in the world. If God is one who punishes us for our very being, we will live our lives in fear, not venturing to grow, or give up fear and live life dangerously because we have nothing to lose and we believe we are already damned.

If God is one who demands that we give, and give, and give, without contact, without counting the costs, we end up with burn-out, or a sense of our own worth being related to how much we give others, without ever allowing ourselves to receive, or just relax in God's love.

If our picture of God is of one who changes from hot to cold, on a whim, who is not, "the same forever," how is there any security? We respond perhaps, with fear, or live our lives without any sense of stability.

Unfortunately, the metaphor Father, so loved by many Christians, becomes a stumbling block for others, whose fathers were abusive. Or when the only images of God are masculine. It seems simple for a man to know he is made in the image of God. But a woman, or a little girl always must make a subtle shift when she hears that God is Father, Son, Shepherd, King, Lord, and she is made in that image. She senses that she must deny her own sexual identity as a female to know that she too is made in the image of God. When churches use exclusively masculine images of God, they deprive their members of the riches of God.

Unfortunately, there is often a close link between early abuse and spiritual abuse. Partly it is that one who has been abused sexually, in a Christian environment, often receives spiritual abuse at the same time, e.g. "Don't tell your mummy or God will punish you." For others there is the confusing link between love and power when the abuser is a loved family member. Moreover, the subtle knowing that there are some people who have power over you and that it is not wise to resist, gets translated in later life into a fear of standing up to the abuser, or of being in a loving intimate relationship with God.

Some suggested ways through

So, what do we do if we know that we've been abused or are being abused in a church or in a current relationship. How do we work with this?

For many of us the very naming of what is happening is all we need, and we can get on with life and with God. Others may need to confront their abuser or move to a safer church. But for many others, the abuse is too big, and they may need help.

Spiritual Direction or Pastoral Help

We are dealing with very important issues and it is often difficult to see clearly what is going on within our own in a world without a helper. This person needs to be someone you really trust, and you know will not re-abuse you. Often our prayerful intuition will tell us who this person is.

Unfortunately, for some of us the idea of praying for the right person is fraught because of our own image of the God to whom we are praying. When you talk to this person, maybe a spiritual director, take it at your pace. You don't have to tell the whole story at once. It is important that you keep yourself safe.

There are well trained spiritual directors all around New Zealand. Check the Association of Christian Spiritual Directors (ACSD) website for one in your area. You may be drawn to one some distance from you – most now use Zoom.

Journal

Buy a journal. Make sure it is kept in a safe place. Pour out your thoughts and your feelings in writing. Be as honest with yourself as you feel you can be at present. This healing will take time. Give it your time, for it is one of the most important things you can do for yourself.

If you find you're writing the same thing over and over, try another way. Perhaps write an honest letter to your abuser, (don't send it), or to God, or to the most loving person you know, telling them all about it.

Draw, paint, clay, or collage

Choose the color that most suits your mood and start to make marks on the paper. Scribble or draw your feelings. Draw pictures of God, the one you have been taught to believe in and the one in your best moments you know to be true. Put your feelings into the clay.

Find pictures and words in magazines reflecting what you think and feel and make a collage.

If you're drawing, it may be good to draw in lots of safety first. This may be a safe border, a special room, or someone or something that helps you to feel safe and secure.

Use your body.

Put on music that expresses your feelings and move to it. Go to a private place where you won't be disturbed like the hills, or the beach, and tell the waves or the hills what is happening to you. It's OK to yell. God can take it.

Scripture

Take some of the biblical stories that are meaningful to you and put yourself into them. The prodigal son/daughter, the woman with the haemorrhage, the shepherd, and the sheep. Jesus and the children are some I use frequently. Or repeat some of your favourite words, perhaps from the Psalms or other scriptures. Suck them like you do a cough lozenge, e.g. "God loves me."

If the Bible has been used abusively against you, you may need a sabbath from scripture. Find something else that soothes and meets your need for spiritual nourishment. There are plenty of good books out there.

Pray

Take the plunge and pray, "Loving God show yourself to me." Know that the truth does set you free.

Visual Help

It may be that you have a picture or an object that in some ways mediates God's unconditional love for you. I know of people who have pictures of a mother and child, of birds in a nest in the midst of a storm, of Mount Taranaki, of Jesus in the storm, of flowing water that reminds them of Jesus the living water. Put your object somewhere so it can speak its message to you.

Rely on the faith of someone you love and trust

Ask a good friend to hold you in their prayers while you do this journey. Sometimes in our families, one member will tell lies about a parent and stop another member from relating happily. If that parent is really loving, they would do all they can to make good the relationship with the one who has been hurt. If we do that, surely our God will do that even more. God is on your side and continues to long for a good relationship with you. If you can't believe that, ask a friend to believe and pray for you.

Worship in Safety.

For some, to find a place to worship safely is a big issue. In Palmerston North, some of us have set up worship times midweek. We call it Sacred Space. Among those who come are some who have felt abused by their churches.

We try to offer a welcoming space where we are all free to choose whether we want to be part of the activity or not. There is no force or coercion. There are a few words and many of those we do use are in the form of poetry, story, or personal stories. No one tells another what to believe. We are often left with a question.

We use a variety of ways of helping people have their own experiences of God, using their senses, imagination, and various ways of praying. We include a period of silence.

We always give opportunities for participants to talk in either small groups or in large – they can choose. While we are Christ-centered, the images of God are varied and inclusive.

For many it is the one safe place they can explore their relationship with God, without fearing they are likely to be judged and have their experience labelled as wrong.

On the wall in my room, I have a poster of a rag doll being pushed through a mangle. The words are, "The truth will set you free, but first it will make you miserable." I know that from my own experience. The freedom of knowing that God is good, does love me unconditionally, and wants fullness of life for me is worth all the effort.

I pray this will be your experience also.

14 – PCANZ General Assembly, 2018
Keynote Speech

Tēnā koutou, tēnā koutou, tēnā koutou katoa i runga i te ingoa o Ihu Karaiti. Greetings to you all, in the name of Jesus Christ. As I make this speech, I feel quite tearful. As I looked at you, the amazing group of the body of Christ, gathered from all over New Zealand and from the Pacific and even Australia (G'Day mate!)

I feel slightly overwhelmed when I look at our church and having heard so much that has been said about the different ministries that you're all involved in and reading *SPANZ* and all the other stuff that comes through. God is certainly working through us all in such a variety of different ways.

We are the body of Christ in this land, and I thank you individually and collectively for all that you're doing. When Fakaofo the Moderator rang me, and asked, "Margaret, would you speak at assembly?" I said, "Me, what on earth am I going to speak about?" He said something like, "Oh, just God. The way, when we believe in God, we can all work together. You've got half an hour." So that's what I did in half an hour.

God, is for me, as God is for so many of us – absolutely central to our lives, and in every decision that we make. Every way I look at life, I'm hoping that I'm looking through the eyes of God. Because I know that we are all part of the one body. However different our understanding of God is, however different our background, there is only one God, and we in some way, are made in God's image.

We are loved. We are blessed. We are forgiven. That's who we are. Some of us have had a tough time in believing in God, and many of us have left the church. Many years ago, I worked as a sexual abuse counsellor for the Accident Compensation Corporation (ACC). I saw a lot of people there, who were not necessarily

Christian, but many of them were. I just want to tell you about two people. One of them, a young woman who I had known for years. We did the normal sexual abuse stuff, and after a few weeks, I said to her, "Who's God for you?" This was followed by a deep, desperate silence, and then she started to cry. She said, "God is cold, hard, steel, grey." We were silent for quite a while. And then she unfolded that her Presbyterian uncle, who was also an elder, had abused her from a little baby right through. When she told her Presbyterian mother, she was told, "Do not speak about that. I'll wash your mouth out with soapy water." So, you can understand something of how this poor girl's idea of God was formed.

It was very different to my experience of God, and hopefully different to yours. As she left to go home, I thought, you know how the spirits sometimes speaks to us, so I said, "You know, my God is more warm, soft, and pink." It was a stupid thing to say, but it did its work. She went home and she said to her children, aged eight and ten, "Marg's God is pink." The children went out to play and came back in dancing and said, "Next time you see Marg, tell her that our God is yellow like the daffodils." You notice how nature speaks to us.

Many months later, she came to me just before Christmas with tears in her eyes and said, "I've just discovered something about God that I can cope with." I asked, "What is it?" She said, "Well, I was listening to Christmas carols, and I realised that God allowed God's self to become a baby, and I know about babies. I can cope with babies. I love babies, and babies love me." So slowly but surely, she began to recognise the vulnerability of God and the beauty of God. A few years later, I got a letter from her to say, "My God is now a dancing spirit."

I wonder who God is for you? Not the God we necessarily talk about when we're upfront, but the God that you meet down here. How do you experience God?

I'd love for us to have time to talk at the table about it. Perhaps you might like to do it at teatime. How differently God comes to us. Wonderful Jewish Rabbi, Dr Itzhak Shapira, talks about God being like the sun – we are each a ray of that sun, given a task to shine brightly in the world.

Part of the issue around Presbyterian assembly, and any other assembly, is that sometimes my ray and your ray think differently. We each have to work out how to do it. I am fascinated by the way in which God comes to each of us.

I had an interesting childhood, with very good parents, but they seemed quite cold – not warm. They didn't speak to me much. They never kissed me or hugged me. My spiritual director said to me, "Marg, who's God for you?" I said, "I feel as though I'm in a warm, safe place being fed and loved." And she said, "It sounds like a womb." I said, "Ah, I'm in the womb of God."

I went off overseas, but do you think I told anybody around New Zealand that my image of God was the womb? Not on your Nelly. I went overseas to participate in one of the courses with Rosemary, Radford, Reuther, and while there she asked us, "Who is God for you?"

People were saying things, so I thought, Oh, I'm in America – nobody knows me. I said, "Womb." And she said, "Biblical" – and I went, "Wow!" My Hebrew is hopeless, but I discovered that the Hebrew word for womb is *rahim*, close to the Hebrew word *rechem*, which means compassion. When we talk about the compassion of God, the image is of the womb, and we are all in the womb of God

It's still a beautiful image for me – not even an image – it's a feeling for me.

The other way that God speaks to me, is through stories as told by Jesus. You know, all the stories that Jesus told us about creation, the mustard seed, the way of the weeds and the good seed, the hard soil, the soft soil. Lots and lots of stories about creation.

I remember being on retreat one day. It was one of those beautiful retreat places where there's lots of country paths, lots of native trees, but also some of those trees that change with the seasons –

deciduous trees. I walked around the corner and was absolutely struck when I saw a bright red maple with the sun shining on it. God, you're amazing. Look at your beauty! There was something like electricity going through me. It was only when I started to talk to my spiritual director, that I was asked, "Marg, have you heard of Moses?" Yes, of course. "Have you heard of the Burning Bush?" Yes, I had. "Go and read it, will you? See if God's saying something to you?" And of course, that's the call of Moses to free the slaves. As I prayed into it, something that had been very slowly, but at the bottom of my gut, began to come up and it was a new call on my life.

I wonder how many of you have had Burning Bush moments? They might not necessarily have been a Burning Bush, but that deep sense that one minute your life's going this way, and the next minute you are turned around and you know that there's a call on your life, which is maybe very different. Just get in touch with that sense, for a moment, of the times when you have felt that call of God to do something that's unexpected, but that you know, that you know, that you know, that you know is who you really, deeply, are. This is not something that your mother or father said that will make you good, but something that is integral to the you that is. Just have a few moments as you are in touch with that.

Now, God speaks to us in so many ways. On one of the Spiritual Growth Ministries training courses, we were sent out to have a contemplative walk. It was one of those very quiet strolls with your eyes open, your ears open, your nose open – being aware that God may want to speak to you through creation. Suddenly, I was stopped, by a tree that had been hit by lightning and was instantly struck by something that had happened in my own life, which was very early sexual abuse. Ah, and then this little voice inside me said, "Surely, he has borne our griefs, and carried our sorrows." And, then I knew that God knew what I was going through.

I wonder how you open your heart to God – obviously through the scriptures. Probably the most basic, wonderful way that we hear God, is through each other. Sometimes it's through somebody who you really don't like, and who you think doesn't listen to God. "Their God is not the real God. I've got the real God inside me!" But sometimes you are shocked into hearing the truth through their own lips.

I wonder how many of us choose to go out for a walk, perhaps first thing in the morning, to listen to the birds, to look at the trees, to be overawed by the beauty of the majesty of the clouds, and the sky or the sea. Wherever you live, be open to the fact that God may speak to us. Our God is longing to communicate with us, absolutely longing to communicate. Often, we're so busy running around doing God's work that we don't have the time to stop.

The other thing that I know is deeply part of my spirituality and is probably part of your spirituality. When I am doing something, being called to do something, or going through an interesting time, I say, "Jesus, remind me again about how you feel about this, what's happening for you." Often, as we do that, it's as though Jesus is reminding us of all the times, for example the times when I look very extrovert – and I am, but I long to be by myself – and I feel the need to rush off and to be outside somewhere. One day as I sat with the scriptures, I opened the pages and I just kept on seeing how often Jesus needed to get out and away from the people. He even walked on the water. I tried that, but it didn't work.

Going off to the mountains, going away from the disciples and to have that sort of conversation with our own Lord about, "Is it okay for me to take time out?" And I certainly want to wave my hand about Spiritual Growth Ministries. If you are thinking of becoming a Spiritual Growth Minister, or a Spiritual Director, please go onto the website.

Do you know the history? One year, in Gisborne, Presbyterian ministers, John Franklin, Shirley Pyper and Presbyterian elder Anne Hadfield, all got a sense of hearing God saying, "I want you to set up a retreat where you Presbyterians can shut up." (I'm sure that God didn't use those exact words!) Anyway, they did that. And then thank God for Lester Reid and the Parish Development and Mission Department, who gave the first amount of money to set up the Spiritual Growth Ministries. This happened as ordinary people, listened and responded to God. Now, if you go to any of their training events, you find Catholics, Anglicans, Pentecostals, and Presbyterians, all learning how to listen at depth and help people explore what it means to be open to God.

What is the call on your life today?

I've been absolutely fascinated as I have listened to people, thinking, oh my goodness. Thank you, God, that you never asked me to be executive secretary or in charge of finance or the book of order. God knows me, and God calls me. God knows you, and God calls you to do what is the most life giving for you, and for the community of all people.

So, what do we do, when we're sitting in assembly and we're talking about something like euthanasia, or in my days, homosexuality, or the marrying, or the blessing of same-sex marriages? You know, some of those contentious things – or are they not contentious anymore? When you look across the room and think, "He'll get up in a minute and he'll say something diametrically opposite to what I believe." But somehow, we really, really, need to know, that this person is also a child of God – made in the image of God, just as we are. And okay, some of us might have a little bit wrong, none of us are perfect. But how do we learn to be one body?

I'll tell you how I pray – and it's not always successful. It doesn't always change my heart. I sit with open hands, and I say, "God, you are in me, and I know that. I also know you are in him or her. Help me to see them as you see them, change me and them." So often the prayer is, "God change them, so they believe like me. But please be with us both. Transform us and help us to engage with each other." Often, before I go to sleep at night, I will deliberately put my hands out and say, "God, you know what's troubling me. Please work on me while I'm asleep, while my brain's not quite so active, and help me, transform me, and if necessary, transform that other person, so that when we get to assembly or wherever, we can hear each other, and listen to each other in love."

We won't always agree even then. But somehow, we've got to stop praying, "God, change the other person" – and be willing for our hearts to be broken open with love.

The image that God gave me for myself years and years ago was that I came fresh from my mother's womb, alive and fresh and innocent, and bit by bit, I built a safety barrier around me, around that place. "Margaret, you should never disagree. Margaret, you should never get angry."

You may be different, but I think we all do it. We learn how to get along with our own family, with our own schools, with our own community. And that's very, very, helpful, and very sensible for when we are children. But when we get involved now, as we are, with this important, deep stuff, that God's calling us to, we need to let go of some of those barriers – allow God in to break down the barriers, so that, with the freshness of coming from the womb of God, we can speak the truth, our truths, and hear the truth, because we are all in that womb of God. We are all being fed in that womb. We are all being nurtured and kept safe in that womb. And we are in the one womb, not in many.

My prayer for us all, is that we will deepen our openness and our relationship to God. Take me deeper Lord, take me deeper God. Show me the beauty and the best of you that is in me. Help me allow you to break down some of those barriers that have been so important for my safety but have kept me distant from other people. Help me to be fully your person in this world.

My prayer for us is that we will recognise that we are one people, one people in the womb of God, and be reminded of that lovely Isaiah passage, where God is the midwife, and that the midwife will bring us forth into new life, as a Presbyterian church. I pray for us all, that we will be open to the movement of the spirit within us so that we will be more like Jesus, day-by-day, and open to the enormity of God's love for all people.

That is my prayer for all of us. Kia ora tātou.

15 – Ever-Widening Circles

It's been fascinating to look back on this theme in my life. Perhaps it started as an 18-year-old when I became a Christian in a non-Christian family. Then there was the call to be a Methodist Deaconess, and while training at Esperanza in Melbourne, I went to a Catholic weekend retreat. It seemed natural to me, but it surprised others.

When I met and married Warren, I became a Presbyterian. Although he was a very open man and was a very important part of my openness, at the time, there was no thought of him becoming a Methodist – it's just the way it was.

Over the years I have attended many retreats in New Zealand and overseas. I have also facilitated retreats which have been open to everyone, regardless of one's faith. Some of these experiences I've shared in previous chapters. For example, I was the only protestant, in the midst of a lot of Catholic nuns and priests, at the 30-day Ignatian retreat at Mount St Mary's in Hawkes Bay. I'll expand on my interfaith journey here.

When I was the Director of the Wellington Marriage Guidance, one of our counsellors was learning about Transcendental Meditation (TM). I appreciated what it was doing for her, so I too began to meditate. Being a marriage guidance counsellor taught me to honour both sides of the partnership. A useful tool in many situations.

After Warren died, following a call, I set up our home as a house of prayer – The Still Point. I invited Judith Anne O' Sullivan, a Dominican sister, and Yvonne Munro, a Josephite, to join me. One of my favourite memories was taking Judith Anne with me to a workshop on prayer in Southland after I had been made Moderator. I introduced her, "You will know that my husband has died so I now have two amazing partners. This is Judith Anne who will help us learn more about prayer. Everyone smiled with delight. She is a Catholic Sister." The looks on their face changed very quickly. But once Judith Anne started to talk about God and prayer, everything changed. All these years later, I still think it was one of the more important tasks I did.

This is not traditionally known as Interfaith, but I realise today that the reason I became Moderator of the PCANZ was that the year John Evans was Moderator, he invited me to take night prayer. I had prepared it but realised that there was a lot of pain around some of the sexist language for God and people. As was my usual practice, I tore up what I had prepared and spoke from my heart. Using all I had learnt as I worked with ACC with many women who were survivors of sexual abuse, I spoke of the amazing variety of names and descriptions of God available for us, and how if we are to communicate with each other we need to accept that some words like 'father' only bring up memories of abuse. My final paper for my spiritual direction training at Shalem, Washington D.C. was on, "The effects of sexual abuse on women's naming and experiencing of God."

After the meeting people came up and said, "you need to be our next Moderator." Although this was not on my wish list – I later became one.

Then in 1995, as Moderator, the most dominant issue was the gay one. Once again it felt like two different religions talking past each other. Often with that same sense of mistrust and denial of the others' – "true faith" – with scripture quotes being bandied about to prove, "We are right, and you are wrong."

In the meantime, my son Mark went to the Kinmount Buddhist Centre in Canada and became deeply involved there. Returning to New Zealand he went to Wangapeka in the South Island. Wangapeka – a non-sectarian retreat centre – is a place to study, "Wisdom, Compassion and non-clinging awareness." I was told by one of his friends that Mark had seen such a change in me, that he knew he needed to learn to meditate, and he's now teaching at Wangapeka.

By this time, I'd been leading Christian retreats for many years and decided I needed to go for a month-long silent retreat. It was interesting being the only Christian in the group but at the end, when we were talking, I discovered that most of them had grown up Christian but had moved to Buddhism because it helped them go deeper. As the teaching happened, I found my self saying, "Yes, Jesus said that, but he said it this way!" Since that first retreat at Wangapeka, have frequently returned for more retreats.

In later life, I had given up most of my preaching, when I was approached by Fakaofa the Moderator to be. He asked if I would address Assembly 2018 on, "Who is God and how do we become one body when we have such different beliefs." He said, "You have half an hour." I thought, "Oh yeah!" – I think God spoke through me. I've shared the text of this address with you in chapter 14.

Nowadays, in my spiritual direction work I am aware that the scriptures I use most often are those where Jesus welcomes the ones on the edge or chooses to go against some of the Jewish laws for example:

- The Samaritan woman

- The leper

- Matthew the tax collector, the woman who anointed him, feeding the disciples on the Sabbath etc.

A very inclusive ministry.

I am aware that through my ministry years I had little thought for people of other faiths, except the Buddhists.

Just before the Christchurch Mosque massacre in March 2019, when I had just turned 80 years of age, I was praying, "What now God?" The answer clearly came – "Interfaith." I really did not know what that meant or what to do, but sensed God saying I will point the way. Since then, I have made friends with two Muslim women and had in depth conversation with a Hindu market stallholder about life in India and the relationship between Hindu and Muslim people and faiths. Somehow, I keep finding myself amidst very racist conversations. I heard a woman in the (in the swimming pool) suggest, "Those Muslims should become more like the Indians! The Indians came here and wore their saris, and after three years they dressed like us." My response was, "So, should we have chosen to be more like the Māori?"

"No why?" she replied. "I am a Christian – they worship Allah, we worship God!" And frighteningly she went on, "If they stopped wearing those things on their head they could stay, but it would be better if they went back to where they came from!" I've heard lots more comments like this, which tear at my heart.

Then gifts happen, like receiving the book, *The World Wisdom Bible: A New Testament for a Global Spirituality*, by Rami Shapiro. This is the most exciting book I have read for many years. In brief, Shapiro gathered a group of scholars from all the faiths and looked at the Wisdom parts of their Holy Books. Chapters like: *Ultimate Reality, The Eternal I, The Way, Living Wisely,* and *Dying Wisely*. It is an amazing prayer inducing, life affirming, book. I wonder if we can use it as a way of talking to each other in small groups. In later life, I still have lots of questions. Where is this leading? I do not know, but it feels both important and life giving for me, as I live through my 80s and I continue to say my, "Yes."

Here's a favourite story I first heard in a meeting of sexual abuse counsellors from someone who works with the abusers.

> We are all sitting around the table up in heaven. The bread and the lamb have just come out of the oven and smell delicious. The wine is sparkling. We are waiting wondering why Jesus is not blessing the food so we can get on with eating it. Finally, he rises from his chair and runs to the door of heaven and with a voice full of joy says, "Judas, Judas, thank God you have come. We have been waiting for you to join us."

It's been fascinating for me to reflect on this particular theme in my life.

Thank you, God.

Wangapeka Retreat 2012

I had a magnificent time on this retreat and returned home in a very meditative mood. Only once, in the middle of it, while I was struggling with Pal (the Buddhist language) and the eastern symbols, did I say to myself, "Next time I am going to do an Ignatian 30-day retreat." But the feeling passed, and I immersed myself in the beauty of the Wangapeka, the depth of the teaching, and the amazing methods of going deeper.

Tarchin Hearn, a Canadian, now living in the Coromandel, was our teacher. Apart from being a Buddhist scholar, he is an ecologist, biologist, botanist, student of the human body, philosopher, poet, and musician.

On the first day, when I was feeling different both in age and in faith from the others, who were all Buddhists, I sat opposite a guy from the U.S.A. Within a few minutes we were discussing Richard Rohr and Thomas Merton. His second kindness came the next day. When we were supposed to be in silence, he said, "Did you know you snored all through the mediation?" What a gift. I had been laying down as I had a sore back, but I chose to sit after that.

At the beginning of the retreat Tarchin asked us what our aspiration was for the month. It was the same question that Alexander Shaia had posed in Wellington. I said, "To dance naked before God." In this context, as my theology was deepening, I said, "To dance naked in God" – hoping to get rid of some of those things that stop me being truly open and vulnerable.

Amazingly, a few weeks later Tarchin quoted from some Buddhist scripture the tradition of dancing naked before God; living without our conscious thoughts covering us. The other theme for me was learning how to be dependent as I got older.

I walked one morning early. It had rained and the trees were singing, the birds were whistling, and the ground seemed to welcome me. I realised how I would not be alive unless I was held by all of this. There were other synchronous moments. Prior to this retreat I had been living and praying with the theme of generosity, without realising it, this was one of the retreat themes. I had taken David Whyte's poem, *Coleman's Bed* from Shaia's book. It was another of themes that were almost identical to Tarchin's in those first few days.

The daily routine of the programme was to:

- Get up early and explore the dark.
- Be still to hear the dawn chorus and wait expectantly for the dawn to arise.
- Go up the hill to the whare at 6.16am for Puja (morning prayer).

- Breakfast at 7.30am.
- Class at 8.30am.

Once we got into it we were having class at 8am. It was a shock to my system, but I got used to it, and went to bed soon after dark.

I loved the Puja. It was full of words like, "taking refuge in compassion and wisdom," and "non-clinging awareness." It also had lots of silence built in. Often sentences were reiterated, e.g. "We do this for the sake of all beings."

One of the major themes was how interdependent we all are, from modern humans right back to the very beginning of life. As Carl Sagan, the great cosmologist said, "If you want to make a cherry pie from scratch, you must first create the universe." Tarchin urged us to, "Contemplate the spacious openness of interbeing." The more he spoke, the more I heard myself saying, "We call that God." Like a shockwave I heard myself quoting Colossians 1:15-19, "Christ is the first born of all creation, for in him all things in heaven and earth were created... For in him all of the fullness of God was pleased to dwell." And then John 1, "In the beginning was the word and the word was with God.... all things were made by him."

Most Buddhists talk of attaining emptiness – Sunyata. Christians, as Cynthia Bourgeault suggests, describe it as 'fullness.'

Tarchin's favourite tool was a microscope, which we all spent time with. He used it to show us the amazing diversity and intricacy of nature. When I picked a toadstool, I put it under 160 times magnification and was amazed to see the number of beautiful little translucent, silver creatures scurrying around. The toadstool itself had the most delightful convolutions. Another day I gently extricated a spiders nest from its safe home and looked. I was awestruck as I perceived what looked like a pregnant woman's belly writhing around, and minutes later an arm came out. I prodded it gently so I could get a better look and it stopped moving! I came back later, and it had died. Mea culpa! I felt deep sorrow.

The retreat started with 21 people. Some left after the second and third weeks. For the final week there were 16 in the group ranging in age from 19 to 73 – guess who the oldest was. I felt surprisingly free to talk about my Christianity. Tarchin used words like God, and grace. He quoted Jesus and, *The Cloud of Unknowing*, and Eckhart, and Gendlin, focusing very aptly and in context. I often found myself saying, usually to myself, "In my context I would say the same thing, but I would use these words."

I was aware of a very familiar lump in my tummy. As I breathed into it, with all the help given, I discovered that I was holding on to the fact that I hadn't been as good as stepmother as Maria von Trapp in *The Sound of Music*. This film came out the week I went back to the Methodist Ladies College and told the girls I was going to marry a man with seven kids. I realised that I'd been holding on to that for 46 years! I got very angry at poor Maria, until I realised it was not her fault. MGM or Rialto had done a brush up job, and she probably had her very difficult times too. So, I exerted a little anger at the film companies, and then forgave myself. Obviously, I kept remembering lots of times after that. I feel that it is continuing process, this living gently with oneself.

We had Sangha (community) sharing about once a week. I was going to tell them about all my birthing dreams, but instead lay on the floor, (they would call it prostration). Suddenly, I had the picture of the way the Tasman meets the Pacific at Cape Reinga, and the turbulence in between. I spoke of having grown up in the Christian sea. I learned to swim and to teach others to swim and to dive very deeply. But I had now crossed into another sea, and was having to learn new strokes, and new ways of being, but the ocean was very familiar. The way I had learned to be was so translatable to this sea, in fact they are the one sea.

For our final sharing we had Wonkur – which is highly ritualised and amazing fun, with all the bells and whistles, incense and sprinkling with water. We were called forward to, "Take this bread," (unbaked). Tarchin held it up high and said to me, "Marg you have to grab it with both hands." Something went through me. I knew that I had to move more deeply into what this meant. When people left the whare, I lay on the ground and I shook and shook, and then sobbed and sobbed. Then I saw a beautiful picture that was basically saying, "There is only one sea, there is only one land, there is only one sky. There is only one universe and there is obviously only one God."

I guess I have known that forever, but my body had obviously been holding on to many separations.

I was fascinated, when we came out of silence, by how many people thanked me for my part in it. Many wanted to tell me about their relationship with the church, (not always very healthy). I was astonished to learn that some were interested to know if Christians had retreats, and were surprised when I described the Ignatian 30-day retreat. One young man said he would love a spiritual director, and thought some of his friends may be interested in the retreats. I sent them copies of the websites and gave them contacts they could follow up on.

In her book, *The Barn at the End of the World: The Apprenticeship of a Quaker, Buddhist, Shepherd*, Mary Jane O'Reilly suggests that Buddhism is a practice rather than a belief system. You can sit (meditate), and still be a Christian, or a Jew, or an atheist. I fully agree. I realise that I go to Wangapeka, partly for the beauty, and the four weeks silence, but more than that, for the wonderful meditation skills that I learn – which are so easily translatable – and to experience that all-encompassing sense of the mystery and bigness of God.

This is a poem by Tarchin Hearn.

Dwelling in a space of love,
tendrils of curiosity reaching forth in all directions
we feel our way
softening and sensitizing into the richness of community
a living world within us, around us, and through us.

Apprentices of wonderment and awe,
probing and questioning,
sampling and savouring,
with calm abiding and vivid discernment
together exquisitely intermeshed,
we touch our home.

This world of you and me, and all of us together,
Precious
beyond words.

The ASCD Conference in Christchurch August 2013

While at this conference, I saw a picture on the wall at the entrance to College House. It's called, *Menagerie 2*, by the artist Joanna Braithwaite (Rosemary's daughter). I have added the kererū flying out. (See photo section)

I had previously dreamed of the painting three weeks prior and made absolutely nothing of it except that the birds were vibrant and alive, but not moving far.

Each time Megan McKenna, the speaker, told a biblical story the words that jumped out at me were, "After this Jesus moved on," or "Jesus left that place and went," or "After eight days Jesus moved on."

When Susannah asked us to embody what the message of the last few days was, I became a bird and happily flapped my way through the group that had formed, and then knew that I needed to fly outside.

Many at the conference either saw or heard me sobbing.

I then knew, or hoped I knew, that I need to keep in touch with the group, so I 'flew in' and grabbed Barb's hand. Then Trish came and held me while I sobbed. Then I 'flew out' again.

Later Phil told me I was a kererū, which was amazing as this is my spirit bird. I am enthralled by them and long for them to visit my garden. When I asked what a kererū meant in Māori he said something about integrity, which sounded good to me!

At the time, I had no idea what this meant in terms of my life. I was sure it didn't mean to move from here to there. It was probably something to do with my interfaith journey, as I was aware that the only times I spoke in the group was about Baptism, Eucharist, and Interfaith discussions.

I sent my reflections to Rosemary Braithwaite a spiritual director, who sent it on to her daughter. Joanna Braithwaite replied,

> "That is amazing that your friend had seen the painting in her dream… It is so rewarding when someone responds to a work like that, especially since those works were very much about states of mind. Some of the paintings in the series, which I called the *Hover Series*, had floating figures, covered in birds or butterflies. I hoped that these the paintings might make people wonder what it would be

like if they were able to acquire the attributes of a bird or a butterfly, and in doing so to achieve a higher mental plane. The work at College House is a hovering cluster of birds suspended in the sky… I guess when painting it, I was thinking about the bird's energy and colour, suspended for a moment in time, clustered together and yet free to fly. I love the idea that in a painting you might be able to make something that is not really possible or believable, but in some way still tunes into the subconscious mind."

It's about us all. I knew I had to move away from my well-known circle of friends and activities, to answer God's call to something bigger and more inclusive. The painting *Menagerie,* with the kererū flying out, illustrates this call.

On praying with it since, I have realised it is a vibrant moving group of living creatures, but I know that there is much more happening outside the group, and that is where God is calling me. Richard Rohr's ever-widening circles reminds me of being at one with the universe – with nature. My centre is still very much within the Christian Church, and centred on Jesus, but is now much more inclusive.

I found this piece of driftwood on Waikanae Beach. (See photo section)

It's another reminder of ever-widening circles in my life.

Wangapeka Retreat with Tarchin Hearn September-October 2013

I went to my retreat at the beautiful Wangapeka knowing I would see the kererū, as I had been overwhelmed by their presence last time. I knew exactly where I would see them – in the bank of wintry trees just near the gate – but when I looked, they were not there! How often do we go looking for God where we expect God to be, rather than being open to the mystery? God is far bigger than that!

Kererū

> I came to see you kererū,
> big bulky kererū.
> You fascinate me exquisite bird.
>
> You eluded me for four days
> apart from the sound of you flying overhead.

I expected to see you where I had seen you before,
in the big dead looking trees near the gate,
but you weren't there
and today you appeared.

Were there 13 of you or more?
Still, absolutely still,
not moving.

I wanted to frighten you to see if you'd fly.
But you are too precious to do that,
I walked to the river
and on coming back not one to be seen!

Then with a flap of the wings there you were.
Into the gum tree! Oh bliss
And then another and another and another.

Is this yet another coming together for me
the Eucalypt and the kererū?

I spoke in Sangha sharing of you as a John the Baptist figure pointing me away from self to the Christ. As we walked slowly with Jamie one day, I heard you, just one of you flying overhead. But I did not see you. Instead, my eyes lighted on a cobweb that was translucent with dew drops, rainbow like in the early morning. Bliss.

Kererū 2

I need to write about you again Kererū,
You have become a symbol of God for me.

A glimpse of the ineffable mystery
You appear so unexpectedly
As when Tarchin was speaking and you appeared
just outside the window,
"Marg are you aware?"

I look for you in all the old places
The stand of trees near the road and you aren't there.

But suddenly when least expected you fly past
often with your mates, flapping your wings so loudly
"Are you listening Marg?
Are you aware?"

The moment I say "this is where you'll be
This is how you will look,"
you break open my boxes and say,
"Marg, Marg, listen look, breathe,
Smile, be aware!"

On the last morning when we were doing our exercises with Jamie, all in silence there you were with three of your mates. (Yet another symbol of the Trinity). The whole group heard and saw and delighted with me in you. It felt like Pentecost experience with all of us being in one place overwhelmed by such an unexpected happening.

I know the bible speaks of the Spirit as a dove and the Celts as the Wild Goose, but you my lovely Kererū are my symbol of the Spirit constantly appearing unexpectedly to say, "Marg are you listening, are you watching, are you aware?"

I went on to Tom and Renata's home in Nelson, and on the last day, with time on my hands, I wandered down a side street and came upon Craig Potton's Gallery. Beautiful! But in the back room what was there? Joanna Braithwaite's pictures and a very helpful woman who showed me articles about her work, mentioning people like Teilhard de Chardin! And so in tune with all that Tarchin had been saying.

When I arrived home, I sat to watch the news for the first time in weeks and there was Jim Hickey with a full screen photo of you, amazing Kererū.

You obviously have lots more to tell me.

Then, on my computer all my photos flashed randomly, including one of my grandson Zebedee with a Kererū at Nga Manu!

Back to the dream I'd had three weeks prior to the conference, and to the original need for me to fly free, at what felt like great cost.

As I looked at Joanna's painting, I had been bothered by the bird's proximity, wanting to give them all some space! I realise this is working for me on several levels, with my growing need for space. My extroversion gave way to quite a degree of introversion.

On that retreat, a large part of my work was welcoming parts of myself, that I had not acknowledged, into my heart to tell them they are loved. The other was me needing to welcome people in my past and my present saying, "You too are part of me. Thank you for being you and teaching me so much."

I wonder if one day I will "all come together," and fly free like the Kererū announcing my presence when and where I choose?

On the broader front, the painting expressed the unity of all of life, living and dead, from big bang to outer space, in a continual flow of interconnectedness.

Wangapeka Retreat 2020

I have always enjoyed being at one with nature in contemplative spirituality. While on retreat at Wangapeka, Chani Grieve, an amazing Buddhist teacher, led an evening meditation. We were asked to go out into the beautiful grounds, find a spot that appealed to us, lie down, and with our bodies, minds and hearts, be at one with nature. Following the instructions, I lay down and looking around me appreciated and connected peacefully with my surroundings. Afterwards, we re-grouped in doors. There was no discussion, no sharing of our experience.

The following day we were asked to reflect on the meditation we'd undertaken the previous evening and write about it. I couldn't for the life of me think what to write. Taken aback, I didn't think I had anything to write about. But in the silence that ensued, the words just seemed to flow on the page.

> The good news on God's call to be one
> The earth's deep breathing and I am part of it.
>
> Lying flat on the solid ground, feeling myriads of life forms
> moving around me, under me, about me above me.
>
> Feeling the trees swaying, the birds singing,
> the wind gently blowing,
> Seeing the beautiful blue sky with the fluffy cumulus clouds.
>
> So lovely stretching out to the North and South, East and West.
> Noticing arid deserts
> Snow-capped mountains
> Wooded fields
> Beautiful lakes.

The places where we've devastated the land, the seas,
the lakes, the forests
The shining gems of people working
to call us back to fullness of life.

The wars, the killings and lethal devastation over religion,
over land, over our rights and not yours.

The Trumps and the Putins and the Johnsons,
Xi Jinping's and Kim Jong-uns,
those who follow because it suits them best.

Those of us who cry with pain and frustration.
Those whose lives have been devastated by others.
Those who give their lives, and their love,
and their breathing for others,
for peace for saving of the earth,
for the unity of Spirit.

And the earth still breathes.
And I am part of it for good and for evil.
And God is, whether called Yahweh, or Allah,
or Vishnu or Ganesh…

May we meet together in unison, for the sake of our planet,
and all the people in it, delighting in our differences,
and exploring them together.

Determined to be a small part in the wholesome healing,
breathing of this beautiful planet.

And we remember and are grateful for Buddha and
Mohammed, and Jesus, and Gandhi, and Martin Luther King,
and Emily Pankhurst, and Thic Nhat Hanh, and Mother
Teresa, and Greta Thornburg, and Whina Cooper,
and the greenies, and those who work for the refugees
and crippled children.

And all those who teach and nurture and love and give
themselves for others.

And we pray in our own way.
"Give us the sight to see You in everyone
To see their beauty, their love, their loss.
To let go of our need to be superior,
and comfortable, and have it all.

So that we become love like you,
Servants like you
Bringers of peace, like you.
Until we see all others as our neighbours, as our family,
as one of us.

So that we all, the mountains and the rivers,
the seas and the lakes, the forests, and the cities,
the rich and the poor, the able and the disabled,
the old and the young,
all breathe together with you
in the deep rich breathing of the earth."

Sometime after my 80th birthday, I was praying, "God, what now?" And as clear as the day the answer was, "interfaith." Of course, this journey started a long time ago, but this felt like something new.

I did a little googling and then waited. I had already made contact with the daughter of one of our residents at Parkwood and we had a Muslim contact. Then, talking with one of the staff in a coffee shop she said, "I am an accountant in Hamilton, and I've never told anyone I am a Muslim. After the horrors of 9/11, I decided I needed to wear my burka to work and say, 'I too am a Muslim. All Muslims are not terrorists.'" One day, she said to me, "I've decided to wear my scarf… on bad hair days!" We both laughed.

Apart from the Christchurch horrors, I heard an enormous amount of racism, that disturbed me. I planned to go to the Kilbirnie Mosque and wasn't sure where to get off the bus. I asked a man who sat close by, and he said, "Hi, I am a member of the New Zealand Interfaith Council. I am a Hindu." He offered to send me details about the Wellington group.

I was warmly welcomed at the Mosque by so many beautiful women. It was a powerful experience filled with love, and gratitude. I read the posters on the wall about Mohammed and Jesus, and a young woman gave me a copy of the Koran!

Never say 80 is too old! I later set up a wonderfully diverse Interfaith group and we met to get to know each other and worship together. It was amazing!

The ever-widening circle continues to expand.

16 – L'Arche

Following the call to sell The Still Point, I sold my home and moved to Waikanae Beach. I looked at 95 houses before I found the perfect one for me at 25 Toby's Way. My new home was just four and a half minutes' walk from the beach, with good neighbours, good community, views of Kāpiti and the hills from my bedroom, an external counselling room, a lovely garden… and of course, much closer to the family in Wellington.

With a change in lifestyle, I took up two new activities – learning to paint, seeing the world with new eyes, and learning to play golf. I enjoyed both activities immensely and met some fascinating people.

Leaving behind the home and garden that Warren and I set up, friends, ministry and wonderful faith communities, wasn't easy, but I had a sense that God was in it all and I needed to wait and be open to where the journey leads me.

While my greatest loss was the friends and small groups I was able to share my faith with, I continued my work in Spiritual Growth Ministries (SGM) and undertook a little work in the local parish. I soon discovered two very different communities. One is Kāpiti Uniting Parish; a wonderful progressive group of older people like me. Another is a fascinating small group that provides me with a growing number of friends and contemplative worship. And then I sensed a call to my life as Pastoral Minister with L'Arche, an ecumenical community of people with and without intellectual disabilities. Young and old, some Christian and some not, some of whom have intellectual and physical disabilities, and those with PhDs, all in a community together. This is the L'Arche (The Ark) community.

Founded in the 1960s by Jean Vanier, L'Arche grew out of the Catholic Church in France and is now an international organisation with 135 communities worldwide. Some of you will have read about it through the writings of Jean Vanier and Henri Nouwen. They developed into strong ecumenical, and most recently interfaith environments, with a deep conviction of the unique value and gift of those who live with intellectual disabilities. Assistants share the life of core members of L'Arche communities. For both core members and assistants, it's a challenging and rewarding life.

I attended a retreat for retreat givers at Trosly, the birthplace of L'Arche in France. The theme was how we support and encourage people to grow spiritually in an interfaith community, many of whom have no religious background at all. One afternoon, we had three speakers: our Muslim assistant Nadia, David a Jewish man, and Noel, a humanist. They all told their stories of how they'd become involved with L'Arche, often for a short time, and often as part of a university placement. They found life there and subsequently chose to stay on, some for ten years.

Nadia told the group it was as though the other assistants held a mirror up to her and showed her her Muslim faith. Until then it had not meant much to her, but in a supportive context, she delved deeper and grew to love and respect her faith tradition. "I go to Mass with core members and discover sometimes that God is speaking to me through the priest. There is really only one God. I call God, Allah."

David the young Jewish man, reminded us of our common heritage and asked us that we do not water down our faith. "I need you to be fully Christian so that I can be fully Jewish."

Noel, the humanist, spoke of how delighted he is when the community asks him to do a reflection for the group, honouring his stance and learning from it.

The attitude of each of these young people to life and faith moved me deeply.

The L'Arche charter of 1993 says,

> "L'Arche consists of communities of faith rooted in prayer and trusting God. They seek to be guided by God and by their weakest members, through whom God's presence is revealed. Each community member is encouraged to deepen his or her spiritual life and live it according to his or her particular faith and tradition. Those who have no religious affiliation are also welcomed and respected in their freedom of conscience. Unity is founded on the covenant of love to which God calls all the communities."

I find this a wonderful vision which we uphold in our community in Kapiti. Sometimes it seems like we are small and very vulnerable, though our heart is strong. However, the spirit of God encourages us all to grow in faith, regardless of our nationality and faith background. It is a magnificent community to be a part of.

We have three houses in Paraparaumu, with four core members, two of them in one house, two in another, and a group of wonderful assistants who come from all around the world to live and work with us for six months or more. At the time of writing, our assistants include a Swiss, a Japanese, a German, and one from the Wallis and Futuna Islands, who along with several kiwi core members, all live together. You can imagine the riches and the challenges.

I am overwhelmed at the way in which I learn from those who are most handicapped, about welcome and unconditional love and patience. They are indeed the face of Christ to me at present. Mike Noonan, the regional coordinator challenged us at a council meeting to become a prophetic Eucharistic community to all our churches. His words hit me in a very deep place, and I began to pray and talk and wonder about what that might look like here in Kapiti. Then I had a dream about a birthing woman, a midwife, and me the resistant one who wanted the new life to happen somewhere else. To cut a long story short, for a variety of practical reasons the pastoral minister who is a Catholic priest and offered mass weekly, had to do another job for six months and they invited me to be the temporary pastoral minister. I joked, "That means I will take Eucharist, doesn't it?" We all laughed, but the question is an important one that exercises all L'Arche communities all over the world. Many of them are interfaith and they struggle and live with the ecumenical reality of all that. Very exciting.

Being their Pastoral Minister, was a truly ecumenical task and I loved it, even though they didn't ask me to celebrate the Eucharist! Many years later I wrote an article about this for *Tui Motu InterIslands*.

I recall one occasion when I sat with the assistants at their formation time and asked who God, the sacred, the divine is for them. It was a most holy time as we recalled our own sacred history, told our stories, and listened with great warmth and openness to each other. We discovered more of the creativity of our God. Emmet put his hand on his heart and said, "God is in there."

Night prayer is one of our cornerstones of our life together, when we read, pray, and sing together. The core members take great delight in leading this. One member, Stephen, always makes sure we pray for the armed forces and those who are hungry. There are lots of prayers for our families and the assistants who have returned to their homes overseas.

Easter is always a special time for us. We have one of those 'God Moments' at our Lenten Open Night of Prayer, our window to the community. One of the Easter themes was Journey Towards Jerusalem with Jesus. We set up the road through the living room, right through to the wall of the prayer room, with clothes and boulders. Arahata, one of our houses, was to bring the big cross. We were all prepared, chatting as we waited, when suddenly, there was a deep hush and Kim walked in carrying the cross, slowly wended her way along the road and very reverently, laid the cross against the wall. Worship had begun.

Foot washing is central to our community life. On Maundy Thursday we gathered in the lounge and listened to the gospel story. The bowl was passed around and we washed each other's feet and laid hands on each other and prayed. Peter, one of our core members who lives with Down Syndrome, very tenderly washed the feet of one of our assistants, a woman who had experienced a really hard time. I had never seen anyone do this task more tenderly, and as he prayed for her, he very gently stroked her face. None of us sophisticated leaders could have done that – we just don't do that in public – but he did, so unconsciously. Some of us were in tears. The woman said it was the most wonderful thing that had ever happened to her.

When Michelle, one of our most loved community leaders was leaving us, she joined us for our last Open Night of Prayer together. We chose Ecclesiastes 3, "To everything there is a season…." We broke up into twos and played charades, where one couple acted, "A time to be born, a time to die…," and we all guessed, "A time to weep and a time to laugh," and then we chorused, "and God is with us," after each couplet. It was a wonderful fun night where we truly embodied the scriptures.

In 2014, Candice Wilson came to New Zealand to be the Community Leader of L'Arche Kapiti. Prior to that, Candice, who has a Masters in Divinity and a Masters in Peace and Development Studies, had gained experience with two different L'Arche communities in Canada and had also been a volunteer with the Special Olympics. We are so fortunate she chose to become part of the local community.

I first met Laura when she was a house leader at L'Arche many years ago, and now she is our Spiritual Life Leader. She told me of one of those God given moments when she was praying for direction at the statue of Mary (located up the hill in Paraparaumu), and she came across Michelle Ness, the Community Leader. Having just finished her Psychology degree, Laura was wanting to find a community that celebrated the fullness of humanity. She now also has a Masters degree in Educational Leadership, and a Masters in Theology. She has spent time in Urban Vision, Catholic Worker and L'Arche communities, and is amazingly well suited for her job as Spiritual Life Coordinator.

Jocelyn Worster, who has had lots of experience with L'Arche in Canada, recently joined the staff in Kapiti. She too has studied Theology and the Arts.

I have met Jesus in more ways than I can count, and have discovered a deeper understanding and appreciation of what he was saying, when he spoke of the poor and the children who are the ones who lead us. When I attended a L'Arche accompanier's event in Sydney I learned an enormous amount about the ethos of the organisation and met some startlingly beautiful people. While I thought my life was interesting, I noticed that everyone who spoke at this event was alive and delightful, and had given themselves in so many ways. My involvement with L'Arche continues and is a great cause of fun, hard work and spiritual growth. This work has a very special meaning for me as my great granddaughter Mimi, also has Down Syndrome.

Do you or someone you know want to come and join us? The work includes cleaning, cooking, and bathing, as well as all the fun, delight, and spiritual growth of community. There may also be space for special people with intellectual disabilities. It's a wonderful opportunity to discover more of the unique giftedness of each person, no matter how disabled they are, or what faith they are, and to be ministered to by them through their amazing love.

For more information on L'Arche and how you can become involved, check out this short video clip: https://vimeo.com/478286941/b8e0b30bb2

17 – Old Age is Not for Wimps

Moving to Parkwood

I began writing this 10 years ago when I was 73. I'm now finishing this chapter aged 83.

Twice a week I sit with a group of older women drinking coffee. We have just come from the gym where we are working at keeping our bodies fit.

The conversation ranges over many areas. We are a fascinatingly diverse group. All of us held positions of responsibility in the past, and all have a deep, but varied, spirituality. Almost always one of us will say, "Oops, what's her name?" Or, "I was just about to tell you something important and now I have completely forgotten what it was."

Mary's husband has just had to go into the hospital care unit at the local retirement village because of Alzheimer's. I have two siblings with it.

Jane's going to give up the gym because her arthritis is too difficult to manage. Betty has just had a hip replacement. Two of us are widows.

Sometimes we laugh at what a bunch of crocks we are. There are the very funny but poignant stories. "I lost my keys for three days and do you know where they were? In the tissue box!"

"I went to drink the water I have beside my bed and discovered his teeth in my glass."

But other times, we sit in silence or even cry with each other, as we recognise the growing powerlessness that is happening within us and those we love. What an important time this is for us as we negotiate the rapids of failing bodies and minds. Perhaps this is a time when we can, "Let go and let God." That is not to say that we don't do all we can to eat well and exercise our bodies and our minds, but perhaps this is a time when we can really learn to trust that God is in all and is faithful. That there are, "Treasures in the darkness and riches hidden in secret places," and God still, "calls us by name." (Isaiah 45:3).

"Listen to me you have been born by me from your birth, carried from the womb, even to old age I am God, even when you turn grey, I will carry you. I have made and I will bear, I will carry and will save." (Isaiah 46:3-4)

This is a time to unlearn so much of what we have spent our energy learning. To be successful, to get to the top of the tree, to not show our vulnerability... this is a time to grow by subtraction.

Carl Jung said,

"What is a normal goal to a young person, becomes a neurotic hindrance in old age."

Teilhard de Chardin said,

"In my younger years I thanked God for my expanding growing up. But now I thank God for the grace of diminishment."

That is not an easy task, but I am aware that we need to find God in all this too. It seems like the call is to dismantle so many of the walls we built to survive, the 'false selves' that helped us make our way in the world. To put aside our need to be perfect, to be needed, to always succeed, to be powerful..., that hides the wonderful person that came fresh from the womb of God.

Richard Rohr said,

"Pain teaches a most counterintuitive thing: we must go down before we even know what up is. In terms of the ego, most religions teach in some way that all must 'die before they die.' Suffering of some sort seems to be the only thing strong enough to both destabilize and reveal our arrogance, our separateness, and our lack of compassion. I define suffering very simply as 'whenever you are not in control.'"[4]

"All healthy religion shows you what to do with your pain... If we do not transform our pain, we will most assuredly transmit it..."[5]

"If we cannot find a way to make our wounds into sacred wounds, we invariably become negative or bitter. If there isn't some way to find some deeper meaning to our suffering, to find that God is somehow in it, and can even use it for good, we will normally close up and close down."[6]

Olivia Ames Hoblitzelle, in her book, *The Majesty of Your Loving: A Couple's Journey Through Alzheimer's*, tells the story of when she went on retreat. Struggling with her husband's growing dependence and loss of life, she said to the director, "Everything's falling apart. I want to talk about anger and death." Her very wise director said,

> "You need to feel all of it, your frustrations your anger, your grief and experience your full humanness. Accept that all the old securities are collapsing. It is all going, showing you the process of death. This is the biggest thing you have ever done so you need to be easier on yourself! Just make your life big enough for yourself. Rest in the spaciousness. Let your heart be broken open with love. The centre will hold. The centre is the luminous centre, the great heart, the heart of love."

One of the most important revelations for me when I was with my brother and sister in Australia and watching their diminishment, was my fear of having Alzheimer's. It increased, exponentially. I sensed God saying to me, "Even if you do have it, I will not let you go." Of course.

How do we deal with this stuff? Our own diminishment or that of others? In lots of different ways. Sometimes we go to go to a lonely place and scream, sometimes it helps to get large sheets of paper and draw and draw. Certainly, it helps to find a trusted friend and let it all hang out. Why not sit with God in prayer. Experience all the feelings and invite God to come. Whatever we do, it is important not to push it down and not to become a miserable martyr. Psychology talks about co-dependence, when we give so much, we become resentful and angry. Buddhism talks about the principle of two benefits. For something to benefit another, there must be a balancing benefit to oneself. Like a bird with two wings – Wisdom and Compassion. If it has one without the other, the bird cannot fly. Wisdom without compassion is unsupported by wise action; compassion without wisdom can exhaust us so there is no strength left.

The Prophet Mohammed said, "You must die before you die." Jesus said, "…unless a grain of wheat falls into the earth and dies, it remains alone; but if it dies, it bears much fruit." (John:12-24) Let go, let go, let go, until all that is left is you and God. But of course, we all still have to live with our own fears frustrations weaknesses and loss of those we love.

Perhaps this is one of the most important growing times of our life.

The title of the book that was a lifeline when I spent time with my ageing siblings, comes from the quote by Rumi, "Your loving does not know it's majesty until it knows its helplessness."

So, I pray:

The Serenity Prayer
God, grant me the serenity
to accept the things I cannot change,
the courage to change the things I can,
and the wisdom to know the difference

Benediction
May the Christ who walks with wounded feet,
walk with you on the road.

May the Christ who serves with wounded hands,
hold your hands as you serve.

May the Christ who loves with a wounded heart,
open our hearts to love.

May we see the face of Christ in everyone we meet and may everyone we meet see the face of Christ in us, both now and ever more.

Amen.

• • •

Go as far as you dare,
for you cannot go beyond the reach of God.

Give as extravagantly as you like,
for you cannot spend all the riches of God.

Care as lavishly as you are able,
for you cannot exhaust the love of God.

Keep journeying as a servant,
for God will always be with you.

And know that the blessing of God,
the Father and Mother,
God the son and God the Holy Spirit
will always be with you.

• • •

In 2011, I visited my sister Joan and brother George in Australia. Both had Alzheimer's. I'd witnessed the beautiful care that both families offered to them and the cost.

After seeing my siblings, I came home from Australia emotionally and physically exhausted. As I watched the wonderful yet exhausting care that Sue and Shirl offered to them, I determined that I would not put my family into that position. I decided at that time that I would move into Parkwood Retirement Village, close to where I lived in Waikanae. I did not need to be dependent on anyone or be a burden.

The kids were great when I told them, but wondered whether I was jumping the gun a bit. They asked all sorts of good questions like, "Will you still be able to walk the beach most days?" Since then, I've been very aware of my absolute fear of being dependent, not only when old and sick, but having to ask anyone to do anything that I can't pay or repay them for. I've worked on this in spiritual direction, and supervision. It is obviously very ancient in me. I cannot remember anyone in my family being dependent – we Stirling's were made of sterner stuff.

When I went to my month-long silent retreat in the beautiful Wangapeka, Tarchin the leader, asked us to name an issue we were working with. I named my fear of being dependent, especially on the family. A lot of Tarchin's teaching was on the interdependence of all living things, or as Thic Nhat Hanh, the wonderful Vietnamese peace activist calls it, "Interbeing." I was really interested but deep down I said to myself, "Oh yeah!"

Soon after, I wrote this:

> Today walking up the hill to class
> all the earth is alive.
> Drops on the trees sparkling.
> Clouds moist lifting.
> Ground on which I walk singing with joy.
> Almost forgotten sunlight sparkling and dancing for joy.
> Birds swooping and chortling.
> And me at one with it all.
> Thank you Godde.

I then spent hours thinking of all the things and people I am so dependent on. Whew, the list was long starting with the butcher, the baker, and the many, many people who keep our towns safe. Then the cabbage, the chickens, and the worms etc.

One of Tarchin's favourite quotes was from Carl Sagan, the cosmologist. When asked how to make a cherry pie from scratch said, "First you start with the big bang." Intellectually beyond me but emotionally beginning to make sense.

But this did not shift my fear of being dependent on the family. I worked on this with my supervisor and had very clear images and a dream the next night that I also worked on.

Soon that was to be tested.

One Saturday, I lost half my vision in the garden centre. I was clear enough to know it was not a good thing to drive home. I might have killed all the things and people on my left, and you would be visiting me in prison.

I waited until Monday to ring the doctor, thinking, "Don't disturb busy doctors…"

My reading for the day was Psalm 37, from Nan Merrill *Psalms for Praying*:

> Commit your life to the beloved,
> confident that love will act on your behalf
> Making clear your pathway
> bright as the sun at midday.
> Be still before the Beloved
> and wait patiently in silence.

I rang the Medical Center at 8:00am the following day and was given an appointment for 9:30am. This was miracle number one. I was diagnosed with having a Transient Ischemic Attack, a TIA – which I think means a clot, which could turn into a big stroke if I'm not careful. My mother died of a stroke at age 73, and guess how old I was at the time I had the TIA!

Anyway, dependency test number one came when I was informed that I wasn't allowed to drive home. My wonderful neighbour came with her husband to pick me up and to collect my car. I had two phone calls. One from Wellington Hospital to say I had an appointment at 2:00pm that afternoon with the neurologist. The other from a friend who thought I wasn't looking well and had been aware of me on and off during the night. I asked my friend if she would take me to hospital for the appointment. I might be brave in some things, but this is PhD level bravery for me. I even rang my son Paul and disturbed him at work. He was there at the hospital by the time I arrived, and took notes and cared for me, along with my friend Heather. After much tickling of feet, and playing, "How many fingers can you see? And can you move your arm?" I had an ECG. Then the neurologist reiterated that I was not to drive. I had to wait at home for a scan to check my carotid artery, that was to happen the following Tuesday.

The funniest part was when I read the book on how to live with the fear of strokes. I was already doing everything that was suggested, e.g. not smoking, getting plenty of exercise, etc. The one thing I wasn't doing was to drink two small glasses of alcohol a day!

Later, when I went for a very slow walk along the beach, I suddenly realised the root of this fear. The very little Marg, my younger self, decided that if she demanded too much of her mother, she would run away and leave me. I know that of course my mother would never have done that. But little Marg didn't know that. I became a very good little girl – as independent as possible. It has stood me in good stead up until now, but as old age creeps in I see some of my friends and neighbours struggling with life. I'm so glad I'm working on this.

There is a wonderful quote in one of my favourite books, *The Barn at the End of the World: The Apprenticeship of a Quaker, Buddhist Shepherd,* by Mary Rose O'Reilly.

> I went to the woods because I wished to live deliberately,
> to front only the essential facts of life,
> and see if I could not learn what it had to teach,
> and not when I came home to die,
> discover that I had not lived.
> I did not wish to live what is not life.
> Living is so dear...
>
> *Thoreau Walden*

Multiple visits to the doctors followed. Then a naturopath put me on a very strange diet, which boiled down to no dairy, and no wheat or oats, and a few little things like coffee and alcohol. It felt as if my throat had been cut, but I rapidly saw it as an adventure and began to lose weight.

Shortly after Ben was diagnosed with cancer. At first, they thought it was leukemia, which is what Warren had died of, so we all jumped to scary conclusions. He was later diagnosed with non-Hodgkin's B lymphoma and underwent treatment. I was warmed by the way the family rallied around with both practical and emotional support.

In the midst of all this my brother George died in Australia, aged 85 years. Paul and I went over for the funeral and to see family. In many ways it was a blessing as he'd been living with Alzheimer's for many years, still living at home being cared for by his amazing wife Shirley, who was a nurse. It was a huge funeral with the church packed with thoracic surgeons, researchers, family and friends. As usual at funerals, I learned so much about what he'd done.

The George Stirling Scholarship was established at the Baker Medical Research Institute in Victoria, Australia, as a tribute to his work in cardiac surgery.

Some of my happy memories of George are of walking with him on their farm in Bairnsdale. George loved it there. He had planted every species of eucalypt down one paddock and could name them all. George also painted water colours, taught himself the violin, and learned other languages. He was obviously brilliant and I was surprised when I learned, later in life, that he lived with bipolar disorder.

After the funeral, Paul and I spent some time with my sister Joan, who was also living with Alzheimer's. We had a lovely time swimming and eating and remembering together. My sister's name was Elizabeth Joan, but she was always called Joan. A Physical Education teacher, she was one of the teachers who organised the display at Melbourne Cricket Ground when the Queen visited Australia. Joan was always a very caring person who gave so much to the community and won an Australian prize for ecology. She died not long after our visit.

On my trip home I counted nine kind deeds. These included being served even though I was in the wrong queue at the ANZ, a young man gave me his seat on a bus, and a girl lifted my case for me. I must have looked old and haggard, but I felt so overwhelmed at the kindness people showered on me.

From Toby's Way to Pigeon Grove, Parkwood

On the 30th of April 2014, I asked God the question, as I had many times before, "What is your call God for this next phase of my life?" I recognised I was getting older and more tired. There were questions about work, 'Do I give it up?' Recreation, 'Do I join Probus?' And the final one, 'Do I move to Parkwood?' Parkwood is recognised as one of New Zealand's most beautiful retirement villages, and as such has a waiting list for prospective residents for up to 10 years. Established as a charitable trust, it has a guiding philosophy of providing low density housing within an affordable price range and is managed by a group of professionals who are all volunteers. Residents can participate in a broad range of daily activities, whenever they want to.

Reflecting on whether to move to Parkwood or not, I wrote, "I know in a deep place that you will guide me in, and one day I will wake up knowing it's time to go to Parkwood and put the house on the market." I very quickly gave up all my upfront work, just as I have done in the past when I got too tired.

On the 2nd of May, my Damascus event. I was clearing the weeds in the garden to plant blueberries, and suddenly I knew that I would not be there to eat them. I laughed and laughed and laughed, for I knew that this was God.

Five days later I rang a Real Estate agent with a view to selling my home. I visited Parkwood Retirement Village, where I had my name of the list for years and told them I was almost ready to move.

On the 16th of May, my scripture reading was, "In my father's house are many mansions. I go to prepare a place for you. Do not let your heart be troubled. Where I am you may be too." John 14:2.

I received the first offer on my house on the 7th of June. I turned it down, even though the offer was above the government valuation (GV). Sorting through my stuff, I threw out 50 years of ministry papers. I also had two cataract operations, "that I might see!"

During this time God took me deeper and deeper into who I really am in God. I let go of many of the barriers that I'd put up to protect myself. The theme of my life at that time was let go, let go, let go.

I sold my home in Toby's Way, on the 28th of June 2014 for $70,000 more than the GV! God is in this! And a gift of gifts, as I had nowhere to go, and was troubled as to where I would stay, the new owners wanted to use the house as a rental. So, guess who was the first tenant? Me! The scripture reading for that day was about Peter being released from prison. "My chains fell off my heart was free; I rose went forth and followed thee." – Charles Wesley.

Then a delight of our quirky Godde. The horoscope for the day was, "New things are heading your way, so start offloading. On the home front, why not tackle the cabinets or clear out the garage."

On the 6th of July I saw the house that was to be mine at Parkwood Retirement Village. I loved it and hated it and decided to let it go. It felt old, and tired, and it was so much smaller than I was used to. Is there room for the family to stay? Where can I put my office? Can I really spend all that money on me?

I went back on the 17th of July and realised that it's address is 3 Pigeon Grove. The kererū is my spirit bird and appears often when I need to listen to the Spirit. There were about five kererū near the office when I went back to the village. So many people helped me. Rosemary with all her experience of retirement villages; Betty who came to look at the villa and to support me. Paul and Ben were there, with all their practical knowledge and spatial sense – and they too had seen the kererū! Kathryn, Rosemary Isabel, Bev, and Dyani, who helped me clean and unpack in Pigeon Grove, Parkwood.

I then pondered whether I could spend money on myself; first about buying the house, and then setting it up how I wanted. I recalled with clarity a time when I had eight kids and the potato peeler broke, I said to myself, "Oh well I'll just have to learn to peel the potatoes with a knife!" Can I really spend it on me? Of course, our generous God replied, "Yes. This is important." I had lots of dreams at this time about slowly coming out of a chrysalis, and me taking a group of people into a cave where I had earlier planted something that grows best in the dark. Then gently pulling an amazing little creature out of the dark into the light followed by lots of little chickens.

On the 5th of August, only three days and three months since making the blueberry decision, I signed up for my new home. I wrote in my journal, "Amazing Godde, it has been like floating down a big broad stream. Today it feels like going down a huge waterfall, but I know there will be a beautiful limpid pool at the bottom."

I went to a retreat at the Home of Compassion. Suzanne Aubert, their founder says, "Perfect abandonment of ourselves for the future requires great courage. Let us deliver into the hands of our dear Lord all our care for the future, as well as anxiety about the past."

And then of course the terror as I asked myself, "Have I done a stupid thing? Have I been too quick? Will I survive or will I lose all my money?" And so it went on.

I felt pregnant with the me that Godde wants to birth, as if I was giving birth to the very precious small part of Godde that is me.

David Whyte's poem *Sometime*, became almost a daily reading.

> You come
> to a place
> whose only task
> is to trouble you
> with tiny
> but frightening requests
> conceived out of nowhere
> but in this place
> beginning to lead everywhere
> request to stop
> what you're doing right now
> and
> to stop what
> you are becoming
> while you do it,
> questions
> that can make
> or unmake a life
> questions that have patiently
> waited for you
> questions that have no right
> to go away

I paid my money on the 28th of August, and moved into my new home on the 2nd of September 2014, exactly four months since the blueberry event. Thank you Godde!

18 – Reflections

I've been walking the beach with my friend Jesus and very simply my last chapter came to me. You will remember how difficult it was for me to start this. I did not want to write this book. I was very resistant to you, God, but once I started, I realised what a very rich and varied life I have lived. I remember telling Angela, my wonderful editor, it was going to be a very small book because I haven't done much. Now I have to change that because my life has been very, very, varied, and most of it in response to a call. Thank you God

I'm now very aware that a number of my friends who I used to go on holiday with, or go out with, have died, or are incapacitated. We cannot do what we normally did together. I'm very conscious that this situation may not be far away for me, as I'm living in the moment with an awareness of what older life can bring.

I'm aware of the richness of my life and the variety of my friends, colleagues, and the people I've worked with. What a real privilege that has been. Of all the many things I've done in my life, I know that bringing up eight children has been the most important task. It was probably the hardest and the most gut wrenching, as well as the most delightful and fulfilling. I was on a steep learning curve, and the energy it took was enormous – but I survived. I am delighted and proud of the wonderful adults they they've become.

Jon would frequently travel up to Waikanae. We would have lunch together, go for a long walk along the beach, and have amazingly deep conversations. He became deeply immersed in St Andrew's on the Terrace in Wellington, and was a much-loved member of the parish. The members often spoke of how they enjoyed him offering his 'worm wee' for sale during the notices. Sadly, Jon died of cancer on 28th April 2018. I miss him deeply. He is survived by his daughter Kimberley and her daughter Mimi.

I love the times the family ring or send me a text to check up on me, or to tell me about their children – my grandchildren – or to see little bits about them in the newspapers. We have many family get-togethers, and I love to see how well they all get on with one another. I love seeing their very happy solid relationships with their partners and the wise, caring, loving way they bring up their children. I now have seven children, with seven partners, 19 grandchildren and 15 great grandchildren. There is no need to wonder why it is I feel guilty that I do not do what other people my age do with their offspring. I often feel quite jealous that they have more time and energy to give to them than I do.

I'm now doing very little work, except this book, which is taking most of my energy and time. I have been worrying about why I am never asked to take a service anymore. Of course, my mind went down several negative tracks. I finally said to someone at church, "Nobody ever asks me to preach anymore." She replied, "That's because you keep on fainting." Then I remembered that I fainted once while taking a service. I raised my hands to say, "Let us pray," and landed on the floor. This happened on a couple of other occasions in church. It's also happened in a coffee shop, where several people gathered around to care for me, and on two or three instances, ambulances have been called. Recently a man came up to me as soon as I fainted and said, "Hi I'm a medical officer having coffee over there. Can I check you over for about three minutes?" Later, a woman came up to me and said, "Hi I'm a G.P., can I help?" And then they rang the ambulance. Only twice have I ended up in hospital. In the coffee shop one of my friends said, "That's an interesting way of getting attention Marg."

As I write this, I'm OK. I want to tell you about what's been happening for me here in this lovely safe place of Parkwood. I'm very grateful for the care I get from the nursing staff here, who find the time to pop in and make sure that I'm OK, in a variety of ways. For example, that I can exercise, walk the beautiful walkways, and swim in the pool. I get to know so many fascinating people in this safe, beautiful place.

The interesting thing for me at the moment is to share the idea of dying with many of my friends and neighbours, who are in the process of dying. I can become quite deeply involved. I have two areas of concern:

- Of the actual dying process, and

- What happens to me when I die?

I do not want to die painfully and slowly, as so many friends have done, or are doing. I'm also aware that the family history of Alzheimer's is becoming a scary reality. I forget people's names and do not recognise good friends if I meet them unexpectedly. I do know that whatever happens, you my loving God will be there for me.

I'm going to share information about a couple of books that I've read which have changed my understanding of the dying process. The first was written by Eben Alexander, called *Proof of Heaven: A Neurosurgeon's Journey into the Afterlife*, and the second written by Anita Moorjani is called, *Dying to Be Me: My Journey from Cancer, to Near Death, to True Healing*. Both of these people had amazing near-death experiences, neither of which I'd ever heard of before.

Eben is a neurosurgeon, who was very centered in the scientific understanding of life and death. After his near death experience, his whole understanding of what happens when you die was transformed. He had such a deep spiritual experience of the warmth and the love that was present, that he now teaches a wonderful intertwining of science and spirituality working together.

Anita's near-death experience was very different, but once again it was a warm and loving encounter. She now has the gift of being able to recognise, and hear things that are going on beyond herself in a very unusual way.

Both authors have shared a lot on YouTube and are very popular speakers. If you are interested, check them out.

A third book that came to my attention is, *Dancing to my Death: With the Love Called Cancer*, by theologian Daniel O'Leary. This is an amazingly honest, painful, and joyful account of his living with a painful cancer. Daniel died shortly after he'd finished his book in 2019.

I guess I'm quite fascinated now about the actual process of dying as I've seen too many people doing it very painfully, and very slowly. Yet others slip away so gently. It's not hard to imagine which way I want to go. In a previous chapter I wrote about my husband dying. Warren died very easily one evening, with many of us there. It was a very deep and important time for us as a family. I'm hoping that my children will be able to come to me, one by one, to share with me, and perhaps even some of my friends and colleagues, when my time comes. Before then I will need to revisit my funeral arrangements, which I prepared years ago, and write what I hope might enrich the time for us all.

My relationship with you my loving God, has deepened and strengthened. Each morning I wake very early and use these things from the internet, all solidly based on the scriptures. *Pray as you go*, *Word for today*, and *Lectio 365* – all based on scripture, and all very different, but oh so rich. Some use music or beautiful photos of the natural world from different traditions. My favourite prayer place is walking the beach and opening myself to you Jesus. It can be a place of deep stillness and wonder. I'm so grateful for your gentle voice suggesting, or more often, deep knowing, "Don't say that yet," or "Tell her about…," or "Go this way," or "Try this shop, not that one." All very gently conveyed, and most importantly, "I love you Marg."

What an amazing friend you are. Thank you, God.

Most of my life has been lived in response to a strong sense of call. I am hoping, praying, that my story will help you the readers on your journey.

Bibliography

Fischer, Kathleen. *Women at the Well: Feminist Perspectives on Spiritual Direction.* Mahwah, NJ: Paulist Press, 1980.

Fitzgerald, Constance, OSB. "Impasse and Dark Night," in *Living with Apocalypse: Spiritual Resources for Social Compassion.* New York: Harper and Row, 1984.

Halpin, Marlene. *Imagine That: Using Phantasy in Spiritual Direction.* Wm C. Brown Co. 1982

Johnson, Elizabeth. *She Who Is: The Mystery of God in Feminist Theological Discourse.* New York: Crossroad, 1983.

Julian of Norwich: *Showings.* The Classics of Western Spirituality Series. Mahwah, NJ: Paulist Press, 1978.

McFague, Sallie. *Models of God: Theology for an Ecological Nuclear Age.* SCM Press, 1987

Tribble, Phyllis. *God and the Rhetoric of Sexuality.* Philadelphia: Fortress Press, 1978.

Tribble, Phyllis. *Texts of Terror: Literary-Feminist Readings of Biblical Narratives.* Philadelphia: Fortress Press, 1984.

Vinje, Patricia Mary. *Praying with Catherine of Sienna.* SMP. 1990.

Wuellner, Flora Slooson. *Heart of Healing, Heart of Light: Encountering God, Who Shares and Heals Our Pain: Encountering God, Who Shares and Heals Our Pain.* Upper Room Books, 1992.

Endnotes

1 Excerpts taken from 'The process of call' by Marg Schrader, 'Refresh Journal of Contemplative Spirituality', Volume 11, Number 1, Summer 2012. Published by Spiritual Growth Ministries Trust, Porirua, New Zealand.

2 *Models of God: Theology for an Ecological Nuclear Age* p. 27, ff, SCM Press, 1987

3 McFague p. 33, ff

4 https://cac.org/daily-meditations/transforming-our-pain-2016-02-26/

5 https://cac.org/daily-meditations/transforming-pain-2018-10-17/

6 https://www.saintsophiadc.org/painful-lessons/